The *Waterloo* makes a fine sight as she heads out into Swansea Bay on 1 June 1971. She is heading for Port Talbot to assist the sailing of the Yugoslav cargo ship *Korcula*. The *Waterloo* had been built by Cochrane & Sons Ltd, Selby, in 1954, for service with Alexandra Towing Co Ltd at Liverpool, but was based at Swansea from new. She was sent to Ellesmere Port on the Manchester Ship Canal in 1962 for conversion to oil-firing, after which she spent a short period based on the Mersey. The *Waterloo* then returned to Swansea and continued to put in good service until 1972, when she was replaced by the motor tug *Herculaneum*, and put up for sale. The *Waterloo* was sold to Italian tug owner Societa Rimorchiatori Napoletani, and departed for the busy port of Naples on 14 February as *Dritto*. As such she put in sixteen years' service at Naples, but ended her days being broken up at this port in the summer of 1989.

(the late John Wiltshire)

1

The Britannia Steam Towing Company was established in 1895 and maintained a small fleet of tugs at Swansea. In 1961 R & J H Rea Ltd had approached Britannia with a view to buying them out. To prevent Rea from establishing a tug base at Swansea, Alexandra Towing acquired the business of the Britannia Steam Towing Company in November 1961, together with their last three tugs. These were the steam tugs **Brynforth**, **Graigforth** and **Clyneforth**. The **Brynforth** had been acquired from Clyde Shipping Co Ltd, Glasgow in 1956 with whom she had sailed as **Flying Hurricane**. She was a Warrior-class Empire tug of 254grt completed in February 1942 by Clelands (Successors) Ltd as **Empire Thistle** for the Ministry of War Transport. She was based on the Clyde and managed by Clyde Shipping Co Ltd, passing to them in 1946. Here we see the **Brynforth** at the end of her career, on the bow of Elder Dempster's **Obuasi** in about 1964/65. She passed to a shipbreaker at Silloth in Cumbria in 1965.

(the late Des Harris)

The **Brambles** was the second of Alexandra Towing's former Empire tugs to work at Swansea. She was transferred there from Southampton in 1964 to join **Caswell**. The **Brambles** was a Birch class Empire tug that had been completed by Henry Scarr Ltd of Hessle in April 1942 as **Empire Teak**. She was powered by a 1000ihp triple expansion engine and her boiler was eventually converted from coal to oil firing. Her near-sister **Flying Kestrel** was transferred from Southampton in 1965, and all three Empire tugs were withdrawn from service at Swansea during 1969. In this view in the Kings Dock on 15 June 1968, we see **Brambles** on bow of New Zealand Shipping Company's Sunderland-built refrigerated cargo ship **Tongariro**. After a considerable period laid up at Swansea, **Brambles** was sold to local shipbreaker T W Ward Ltd and demolished at Briton Ferry, during the autumn of 1971.

(the late John Wiltshire)

The **Talbot** was the third motor tug to enter service with Alexandra Towing Co Ltd at Swansea and Port Talbot. She was built by W J Yarwood & Sons Ltd, Northwich, and delivered to Alexandra in October 1961. With a gross tonnage of 153 she was powered by an 8-cylinder Alpha-B&W type diesel of 960bhp, driving a controllable-pitch propeller in a fixed Kort nozzle. After a brief period of service on the Mersey, the **Talbot** moved to South Wales in 1962 to join her slightly older sister ship **Gower**. This photograph was taken at Swansea in the afternoon sunshine of 1 June 1970. In 1979 the **Talbot** transferred to work on a contract at Foynes and was placed under Irish registry, returning to Swansea in 1983. In 1984 she was sold to Avlis Shipping Company and registered at Piraeus. She was soon renamed **Achilleas** based at Volos where she can still be found at work in 2019.

(the late John Wiltshire)

3

Moored close to the entrance of the two drydocks in the Kings Dock are the steam tugs **Formby** and **Waterloo** flanking the motor tug **Talbot**. It looks as though the **Formby** has had her hull painted during a recent drydock visit which may well have been at Port Talbot. The date is 17 October 1969, and within a few days the **Formby** would be joined by her sistership **Canada**. The pair would then be renamed and handed over to Italian owners (see page 7). The **Waterloo** and **Talbot** were still very much part of the active fleet at this time, and it is unclear as to why they are not occupying the usual tug berths at Swansea. Two other steam tugs are just about visible in the background.

(the late John Wiltshire)

The British-built and Italian-owned tanker *Sobrietas* (ex *Tuareg*) of 1953 had been badly damaged while in the Atlantic in February 1970. She arrived at Swansea for temporary repairs and was then sold to Spanish breakers at Vinaroz. This final trip was made under tow from the West German fire-fighting tug *Fairplay X*. This single-screw tug was owned by Hamburg-based Fairplay Schleppdampfschiffsreederei GmbH who had taken delivery of her in October 1967. She was constructed in Hamburg by Theodor Buschmann Schiffswerft, and was powered by a 9-cylinder M.A.N. four-stroke diesel of 1910bhp. This gave *Fairplay X* a bollard pull of 30 tonnes and a speed of 12½ knots. This view of her was taken on 5 March 1970 prior to her departure with the stricken tanker. The *Fairplay X* continued to sail for Fairplay until 1987 when she was sold to Spanish owners Comercio Internacional de Atun SA, and renamed *Tuna Service Dos* under Panamanian registry. In 1990 she began a new life at the Chilean port of Talcahuano for owners Compania Portuaria Talcahuano Ltda as *Naguilan*. Remaining in South America, in 2003 she moved north to Ecuador and was renamed *Isla Santay* for service with Compania Dariem Shipping Line SA, Guayaquil. She was still in service in 2019.

(the late John Wiltshire)

This lovely study of the sisterships *Wallasey* and *Waterloo* in the lock at Swansea was taken in the early evening sunshine on 13 June 1968. As the day fades away these two fine steam tugs are about to conclude the docking of the British freighter *Tongariro* which was bound for the drydocks. After the Second World War, the Alexandra Towing Company continued to place its faith in steam propulsion, and ordered three tugs from Cochrane & Sons Ltd at Selby for 1951 delivery, followed by a further trio for 1954. The *Waterloo* was completed in April 1954 followed by *Wallasey* in June. Each had a gross tonnage of 200,

and was powered by 950ihp triple expansion engine. The *Wallasey* was transferred to Swansea in 1956 and was converted from coal to oil burning in September 1961. Both tugs had left Swansea during 1972, but unlike *Waterloo* (see page 1), *Wallasey* did not see much service after her sale to South Ocean Services Ltd, Portsmouth. She was renamed *Kendiken* in 1972 and spent much of the subsequent 21 years laid up and rotting away. It is thought she was scrapped at Southampton during 1993.

(the late John Wiltshire)

The three new steam tugs delivered to the Alexandra Towing Company in 1951 were named *Canada*, *Formby* and *Gladstone*. These fine-looking vessels were completed as coal-burners and based at Liverpool when new. They had tall funnels which were shortened when their boilers were converted to burn oil between 1956 and 1960. Their masts were also shortened at some point. All three went on to spend periods based at Southampton, and *Formby* moved to Swansea in 1967. The *Gladstone* was sold to Italian owners at Palermo in 1968 while the *Canada* and *Formby* went to Italian owners at Brindisi in 1969. This photograph taken at Swansea dates from 23 October 1969. The *Formby*, now renamed *Poderoso*, has been joined by *Canada* which has sailed around from Liverpool to be handed over as *Strepitoso*. Both tugs would soon embark on the long trip to southern Italy for a new life with owner Fratelli Barretta fu Domenico. They continued to work at Brindisi until about 1988, and were subsequently broken up at the port.

(the late Des Harris)

The **North Buoy** makes a fine sight as she approaches the lock at Swansea on 7 June 1973. Her working days at this port are now drawing to a close. The **North Buoy** and her sister **North Wall** were the only examples of the seven steam-powered "North boats" to work away from the Mersey, while in Alexandra Towing service. The **North Buoy** was also from the small Bowling shipyard of Scott & Sons and had been launched on 11 September 1958. She was delivered to her owner at Liverpool in January 1959. The **North Buoy** had a gross tonnage of 219, an overall length of 104 feet and produced a bollard pull of around 13½ tonnes from her triple-expansion engine. The **North Buoy** also made the voyage to Brindisi to work alongside her sister the **North Wall**. She was graced with the new name **Coraggioso** and lasted until 1988.

(the late John Wiltshire)

Four of Swansea's steam tugs were withdrawn from service in 1969, but that year witnessed the arrival from Liverpool of the **North Buoy** and the **North Wall**. These vessels were significant in that they were the last new steam tugs purchased by the Alexandra Towing Company, as late as 1959 and were slightly larger versions of the three constructed in 1954. This is the **North Wall** on 23 April 1972. She was completed in June 1959 by Scott & Sons (Bowling) Ltd on the River Clyde and was powered by a 1050ihp triple-expansion steam engine. It came as no surprise that when Alexandra decided to dispose of the **North Wall** in 1973, at only 14 years old, she would be snapped up by an Italian tug owner. And so she passed to Fratelli Barretta, Brindisi, and was renamed **Maestoso** under the Italian flag. Here she joined the former **Canada** and **Formby**, and after a respectable second career at Brindisi she was broken up in late 1988.

(Nigel Jones)

The motor tugs **Margam** of 1953 and **Cambrian** of 1960 had left the Swansea-based Alexandra Towing fleet by 1973. The last steam tug **Canning** had somewhat surprisingly lingered on as available for service at Swansea until 1975. In 1976 the local fleet comprised the smaller motor tugs **Gower**, **Talbot**, **Herculaneum**, **Alexandra** and **Rana**, together with the larger **Mumbles**, **Margam** and **Victoria**. The **Alexandra** had been transferred to Swansea in 1965 to replace a steam tug and spent the next 32 years working at the port. She was completed in October 1963 by W J Yarwood & Sons Ltd, Northwich. She had a bollard pull of 18 tonnes and was powered by an Alpha B&W diesel of 960bhp. The **Alexandra** is seen working with **Talbot** at Swansea on 27 January 1976, while docking the BP tanker **British Loyalty**. Howard Smith Towage Ltd took over Alexandra Towing in 1993 and the **Alexandra** was included in this deal. She was sold in 1997 to General Port Service Ltd (GPS), London, transferring to GPS Marine Contractors Ltd, Rochester, in 2001.

(the late John Wiltshire)

The *Victoria* was the last in a series of four large motor tugs for service on the Mersey with Alexandra. All were delivered in 1972 and replaced the last five ship-handling steam tugs on the Mersey. In order of delivery they were *Alfred*, *Crosby*, *Albert* with *Victoria* being handed over in May 1972. All were traditional Alexandra names, the *Victoria* being the second tug to bear this name. She was completed by Richard Dunston (Hessle) Ltd, Hessle, and had a gross tonnage of 272 and an overall length of 107 feet. She was initially transferred to Swansea in 1973 as the third large tug available for use at Port Talbot. The *Victoria* is seen sailing from Swansea on 24 October 1974. She went on to spend many years at Southampton before briefly moving back to Swansea in 1986. She then moved to Felixstowe in 1988 and passed to Howard Smith Towage Ltd in 1993. In 1995 she was renamed *Oakley* to free her name for use on a new P&O cruise ship, and she moved back to Swansea in 3 September 1997. She was sold in 1999 along with *Albert* to Togo Oil & Marine, Lome. They sailed out to West Africa as *Defender* and *Defiant* respectively.

(Danny Lynch)

The *Gribbin Head* was an interesting little tug that visited Swansea during 1991. She arrived in port to tow away the backhoe dredger *Gunfleetsand*. The *Gribbin Head* was new in 1955 to Tees Towing Co Ltd, Middlesbrough, as *Ingleby Cross*. She was built on the River Clyde by Scott & Sons (Bowling) Ltd and was the sister to the *Golden Cross*. Her main engine was a 4-cylinder Crossley Bros. two-stroke diesel of 750bhp. In 1968 she was sold to Fowey Harbour Commissioners and renamed *Gribbin Head* for use at this Cornish port where she worked until 1988. She then passed to Haven Marine Services Ltd, Pembroke Dock, who replaced her Crossley engine with a 16-cylinder English Electric diesel of 1200bhp. By 1990 the *Gribbin Head* was working under the Irish flag for Tuskar Rock Diving Co Ltd, Wexford, her owner in this image. She was eventually renamed *Tuskar Rock* in 1995 and the following year she passed to Spanish owners Pinturas at Huelva. By 2011 her name had changed to *Triva II*, sailing under the flag of Sierra Leone, and she was still active in 2018.

(Mike Aldron)

The **Hendon** was an interesting vessel that had been ordered by France Fenwick Tyne & Wear Co Ltd, Newcastle from the Richard Dunston shipyard at Hessle on Humberside. France Fenwick took delivery of her sister ship **Cragsider**, but in 1977 was unable to take **Hendon**. She was then sold to Alexandra Towing Co Ltd, Liverpool, in 1978 and allocated to the Swansea fleet for harbour and coastal towing. She was a powerful tug with a Mirrlees-Blackstone diesel of 3226bhp giving her an impressive bollard pull of 46 tonnes. The **Hendon** is seen at Swansea on 14 April 1981. Note the towing winch on her aft deck. She was later transferred to Southampton, but moved on to the Gravesend fleet in 1985, where she spent eleven years. The **Hendon** was eventually sold in 1996 passing to Greek owner Karapiperis, Piraeus, as **Karapiperis 12**. By 2015 she was sailing as **Ethy VI**.

(the late John Wiltshire)

In the early 1980s it soon became obvious to Alexandra Towing that in order to be able to compete in the offshore service and construction market they would need to acquire a number of powerful, versatile and seaworthy vessels. In early 1982 they acquired the **Chambon Alize** from Compagnie Chambon, Marseille, and renamed her **Redoubtable**. In 1983 her sister **Chambon Sirocco** was added to the fleet as **Implacable**, while **Chambon Bora** arrived in 1984 as **Indefatigable**. The fourth vessel was **Invincible** acquired in 1983 from Norwegian owners. The **Indefatigable** is best described as an anchor-handling salvage tug/supply vessel of 4690bhp. She was built in Yugoslavia in 1975 by Brodogradiliste Tito, Mitrovica, as **Sea Diamond** for Bugge Supply Ships, London, and passed to Compagnie Chambon in 1980. The **Indefatigable** was initially based at Swansea where she is seen on 26 June 1984. She later moved to Gravesend and was renamed **Avenger** in 1986. In 1993 she was taken over by Howard Smith Towage Ltd and in 1994 passed to West Coast Towing Co (UK) Ltd as **Valiant Nader**. She was once again a regular visitor to Swansea until her sale in 2003.

(the late Des Harris)

The former Port of London Authority Voith Schneider tractor tugs *Plasma* and *Platoon* passed to Alexandra Towing Co Ltd in 1991 as *Burma* and *Dhulia*, and were based at Gravesend passing to Howard Smith in 1993. They both dated from 1965 and were built at Hessle by Richard Dunston Ltd. They were then transferred to Swansea in 1994, and prior to entering service were drydocked. These tugs were built to work in the sheltered waters of London's dock system and out on the River Thames, and therefore had to be modified to enable them to operate more safely in open-water conditions. The *Burma* is seen in drydock at Swansea on 23 April 1994. She soon received handrails above her bulwarks and a complete repaint in full Howard Smith colours. Of interest is the clear view of the tug's single forward-mounted Voith Schneider cycloidal propulsion unit. The *Burma* was then given the local name *Langland* while *Dhulia* became *Caswell*. These tugs remained at Swansea until 1998, after which they were moved around to Grimsby to join the fleet of Howard Smith (Humber) Ltd.

(Mike Aldron)

The small shipyard of W J Yarwood & Sons Ltd at Northwich completed ten tugs for Alexandra Towing up to 1965. The **Herculaneum** was a slightly larger and more powerful development of **Gower** and **Talbot** of 1961, but with her wheelhouse set further back, which gave her a rather untidy appearance. She was completed by Yarwood in December 1962 for service at Liverpool, and did not move to Swansea until 1972. The **Herculaneum** had an Alpha B&W diesel of 960bhp, and featured a controllable-pitch propeller in a steerable Kort nozzle. By the late 1980s two of her forward-facing wheelhouse windows were enlarged to improve visibility and in 1993 she passed to Howard Smith Towage Ltd. In this view taken on 29 October 1993, the **Herculaneum** has started to receive the livery of her new owner, but still retains Alexandra Towing funnel colours. She was sold in 1997 and by 2000 was with Greek owners Ignatios Naftiki Eteria (Michael Spanopoulos SA) as the **Christos VIII**.

(Mike Aldron)

The **Margam** was completed in November 1970 and was the second of the larger tugs ordered by Alexandra Towing to serve the new tidal harbour at Port Talbot. She was of similar specification to her sister **Mumbles**, but had a much lower fo'c'sle and a smaller funnel. The **Margam** was also built at Hessle by Richard Dunston (Hessle) Ltd and like **Mumbles** she also undertook the occasional coastal towing job. She passed to Howard Smith Towage when Alexandra Towing were taken over in 1993. This view of the **Margam** underway in Swansea Bay was taken on 15 October 1994, and shows her in Howard Smith colours, but still advertising Alexandra Towing on her wheelhouse! In 1997 she passed to West Coast Towing (UK) Ltd as **Hurricane H** and continued to work at Swansea and Port Talbot. West Coast Towing were taken over by Wijsmuller Marine Ltd in May 2001, passing to Svitzer Marine Ltd in 2002. The **Hurricane H** was sold in 2007 by Svitzer and eventually went to work in Greek waters as **Voukefalas**.

(Nigel Jones)

In 1993 British Steel awarded the towing contract for Port Talbot tidal harbour to West Coast Towing (UK) Ltd which then set up a base at the port in early 1994. For this West Coast needed more tugs, some of which would need to be large powerful vessels (see pages 34 & 35). A number of smaller fairly new Russian-built tugs were also added to the fleet at this time and included the *Capt I. B. Harvey* which we see at Swansea on 16 July 1994. She was a twin-screw tug of 182 gross tons that was built in 1992 by AO Gorokhovetskiy Sudostroitelnyy Zavod, Gorokhovets as *Vik III*. Upon completion she remained unused, and was sold along with her sister *Vik IV* to Norwegian owners. The pair were renamed *Vic III* and *Vic IV* and laid up at Stavanger. They were purchased by West Coast in early 1994 and renamed *Capt I. B. Harvey* and *I. B. Smith* respectively. The *Capt I. B. Harvey* was not part of the Wijsmuller takeover of ship handling duties at Swansea and Port Talbot in May 2001, and was retained by West Coast Towing for coastal towing etc. At this point she transferred to a new company Valiant Nader Ltd, and was soon fitted with a double-drum towing winch and hydraulic deck crane. The *Capt I. B. Harvey* was then put to work in the Mediterranean supporting a tuna fishing fleet. In 2005 she was sold to Al Jaber Shipping Agency & Marine Works, Abu Dhabi, and renamed *Al Jaber II*.

(Nigel Jones)

The **Salvanguard** was a Japanese-built twin-screw salvage tug that entered service in 1978 with Tokyo Shipping Company and was registered at Uwajima as **Dahlia**. She was built locally at the yard of Kuroshima Dock Co Ltd with a gross tonnage of 2699 and an overall length of 280 ft. As would be expected for a tug of this size, she boasted an impressive bollard pull of 162 tonnes and this was achieved from a pair of 6-cylinder M.A.N. K6Z52 diesels. In 1987 she was sold to Singapore-based owner Sembawang Salvage (VII) Pte Ltd, and managed by SEMCO Salvage Pte Ltd as **Salvanguard**. She arrived at Swansea on 1 May 1996 for drydocking and is seen here on 23 May the day before she departed. In 1998 she passed to Geobay Shipping A/S of Norway for conversion to a seismographic vessel named **Geobay**. She was re-engined and converted to diesel-electric propulsion with a pair of Mitsubishi diesels driving two directional propellers. She was registered in Douglas under the Isle of Man flag, and was still in service in 2019 as **Horizon Geobay**.

(the late John Wiltshire)

The **Trafalgar** was a large Voith Schneider tractor tug built for Howard Smith Towage Ltd of Liverpool in 1998. She was last in a series of eight similar tugs constructed by McTay Marine Ltd at Bromborough on Merseyide. The **Trafalgar** was a bulky tug with a length of 96ft, beam of 39ft and a gross tonnage of 369. A bollard pull of 62 tonnes was achievable and she was also fitted for fire-fighting. When still quite new, the **Trafalgar** was moved to Swansea to assist with a very large ore carrier at Port Talbot, and to demonstrate that Howard Smith could invest in new tugs should trade at the port warrant it. She soon moved back to Liverpool and Howard Smith was eventually taken over by Adsteam (UK) Ltd in 2001. The **Trafalgar** was then renamed **Adsteam Trafalgar** in 2005. In 2007 the Liverpool unit of Adsteam passed to Smit Harbour Towage UK Ltd and the tug became **Smit Trafalgar**. In a somewhat surprising move, in February 2009 she was shipped out to the Far East for an oil terminal contract. She was operating for Smit Kueen Yang at Taipei in Taiwan as **Sky 501**, and was still in service in 2019.

(Nigel Jones)

When Howard Smith took over Alexandra Towing in 1993, the tug fleet at Swansea underwent a number of changes in the subsequent five years that they maintained a base at the port. Towards the end of operations in 1998, the **Albert** is seen at work in the Kings Dock on 8 August. The **Albert** was one of the four tugs new in 1972 to replace the last steam tugs at Liverpool. She was delivered to Alexandra Towing in April 1972 and was a single-screw tug powered by a 9-cylinder Ruston diesel of 2400bhp. She had a bollard pull of 40 tonnes and was fitted with a Kort nozzle. She spent a considerable period based at Southampton from the 1980s where she worked alongside **Victoria**. In 1999 she was sold to Reboques e Assistencia Naval Ltda (REBONAVE), Setubal, and renamed **Mouriscas** under the Portuguese flag. The following year she became **Barra De Aveiro** for Transportes e Reboques Maritimos, Porto de Viana do Castelo. Her name was changed in 2007 to **Barra De Viana** shortly before she was sold to Leopard Shipping Ltd, Gdynia, and renamed **Felis** under the Slovakian flag. In 2019 she was working in the Baltic Sea.

(Nigel Jones)

With the loss of the towage contract for Port Talbot tidal harbour to West Coast Towing in 1994, the closure of Llandarcy oil refinery in 1998 and the steady decline in traffic at Swansea, Howard Smith Towage decided to close its Swansea operation in the autumn of 1998. At this point Cory Towage made a brief appearance at Swansea, and allocated the *Holmgarth* and *Stackgarth* to the port. This shot of the *Stackgarth* is dated 27 April 1999, not long before Cory withdrew from Swansea. Launched as *Eston Cross* on 20 February 1985 by Richard Dunston (Hessle) Ltd, she was delivered to Tees Towing Co Ltd, Middlesbrough, for service on the River Tees. The *Eston Cross* was a twin-unit Schottel tractor tug and the last in a series of seven tugs of a similar design. She was more powerful than the first early examples which were new in 1976 and had a bollard pull of 43 tonnes. Tees Towing were taken over by Cory Towage (Tees) Ltd in 1990 and *Eston Cross* moved to Milford Haven in 1994 and renamed *Stackgarth*. She was soon found to be unsuitable for use at this port and was moved to Liverpool in January 1997, then Belfast, eventually ending up at Swansea in October 1998. She worked at Avonmouth and Portbury from 2000, latterly with Svitzer Marine, and was sold in 2010 to Tuskar Shipping Ltd (Fastnet Shipping Ltd) as *Fastnet Nore*.

(Brian Murphy)

The **Shannon** was completed in October 1981 by McTay Marine Ltd, Bromborough as **Eldergarth**, one of a pair of tugs constructed for overseas service in Angola at the Malongo Terminal at Cabinda. The contract was with Chevron Oil and Rea Towing Co Ltd, the two tugs being constructed for owner S J Murphy & Co Ltd, and placed under Irish registry at Westport. The **Eldergarth** had a gross tonnage of 382 and was the first tug completed by a UK shipyard to feature Z-peller propulsion. Her machinery comprised a pair of Japanese Niigata diesels with a combined output of 3200bhp giving her a bollard pull of 42 tonnes. In 1989 she was purchased from her leasing company by Irish Tugs Ltd. At the end of 1998, the Angolan contract was terminated and **Eldergarth** returned to the UK, passing to Cory Towage Ltd and then Shannon Tugs Ltd, Limerick, in 1999 as **Shannon**. In 2000 Wijsmuller took control, and **Shannon** eventually moved to the Bristol Channel, which is how we see her in this view taken in Swansea Bay in 2001. Later with Svitzer Marine, **Shannon** also worked on the Clyde, and was sold in 2009 to Emu Ltd, Southampton and converted to a survey vessel. By 2012 she was **Safe Supporter I** with STS and based at Lowestoft. She is currently sailing as such in 2019.

(Danny Lynch)

In 1975, not long after Alexandra Towing took over London Tugs Ltd, three powerful motor tugs were ordered for the Gravesend-based fleet. The first of these was **Sun Essex** which arrived on the Thames in July 1977 from her builder Richard Dunston. She was a powerful single-screw tug of 2070bhp with a bollard pull of 35 tonnes and capable of fire-fighting and pollution control. In early 1990 she was transferred to the Southampton fleet while her identical sister **Sun Kent** remained at Gravesend. In 1993 the **Sun Essex** passed to Howard Smith Towage Ltd and was sold in 1999 to Norwegian owner Arne Nilsen Slepebåter A/S, Fredrikstad, and renamed **Big**. In 2002 she passed to Danish owners Jens Alfastsen Rederiet as **Susanne A**. This is how we see her in Swansea Bay on 16 November 2005. The **Susanne A** is towing the tanker **Stella Rigel**, which had engine trouble, from Swansea to Denmark. In 2007 the **Susanne A** passed to Dan Tugs A/S of Fredericia as **Lucas** remaining under the Danish flag. By 2012 she had regained her original name **Sun Essex** and was sailing under Belize registry for Sovlot BV of Zwijndrecht, Netherlands.

(Danny Lynch)

Spectacular lighting over the Kings Dock, Swansea, on 16 December 2001 highlights the rather shabby condition of the Belgian tug **Boxer** as it handles the Belgian-owned spud barge named **Lynn**. This barge was used to remove the experimental Weather Data Tower on the edge of the Scarweather Sands. Heavy downpours were an extra distraction for the photographer this day. The **Boxer** was a salvage tug of 491grt and overall length of 138 feet. She was completed in Belgium by Scheepswerf van Rupelmonde NV, Rupelmonde, and delivered to Unie van Redding en Sleepdienst (URS) in June 1977 and registered in Antwerp.

She was a single-screw tug, her main engine being a 16-cylinder vee-format Cockerill diesel of 4400bhp. This gave her a bollard pull of 55 tonnes and a speed of 14¾ knots. She also featured a controllable-pitch propeller, Kort nozzle and a bow thruster. By 2000 her owner was given as Smit Union Coastal Towage, Antwerp, and in 2005 the **Boxer** became part of what was known as Euro Tugs, a pool of tugs set up by URS and the German company Fairplay. This was to be shortlived for **Boxer** as she was sold to a Ghent shipbreaker in late 2007.

(Danny Lynch)

When a particularly large bulk carrier or conditions such as poor weather dictate, Svitzer will often send a tug down from Portbury or up from Milford Haven to assist with shipping movements at Port Talbot harbour. The ASD tug *Svitzer Gelliswick* has come up from Milford Haven to help out at Port Talbot, and is seen at Swansea on 16 April 2016. In 2008/9 the tug fleet at Milford Haven was completely renewed at great expense with modern vessels capable of handling the LNG gas tankers that would start frequenting the port. The *Svitzer Gelliswick*, new in 2009, was described as a stretched version of Svitzer's M-class and her sisters are *Svitzer Musselwick* and *Svitzer Watwick*. The *Svitzer Gelliswick* is by no means a small tug with a gross tonnage of 490 and a beam of just under 40 feet. Her hull was built in China in early 2008 by Qingdao Qianjin Shipyard, Qingdao, and delivered to the Spanish yard of Construcciones Navales P. Freire SA, Vigo for completion. She is powered by a pair of Niigata 8L28HX diesels delivering 5998bhp driving two Schottel propulsion units mounted at her stern. This gives her an impressive bollard pull of 83 tonnes.

(Mike Aldron)

The ASD tug *Garibaldo* visited Swansea in 2006 and is seen in Swansea Bay on 10 April. She was owned by Purplewater Towing Ltd of Switzerland and was registered in London. The *Garibaldo* was built in China by Guangdong Hope Yue Shipyard, Guangdong. She is designed specifically for tanker-handling, escort duties and is fitted for fire-fighting and pollution control. A large tug at 459grt she has a bollard pull of 60 tonnes and is powered by a pair of Caterpillar diesels developing 4960bhp and driving two Schottel propulsion units. On her delivery voyage the *Garibaldo* towed a barge to the River Tyne before sailing around to Swansea to take stores and give her crew a break. The *Garibaldo* later took up her intended role and sailed out to Sicily to work at port of Termini Imerese east of Palermo. This was on a contract for Italian tug owner Rimorchiatori Siciliani Srl, Palermo, and working alongside another Purplewater tug, *Tigrillo*.

(Danny Lynch)

This tug was on charter to Svitzer for use at Port Talbot, when one of the locally-based tugs was thought to be away for drydocking. The *Thrax* was originally operated by Solent Towage which is a subsidiary of Østensjø Rederi AS of Norway, and provides tug and tanker escort services at Esso's Fawley marine terminal on the Solent. The *Thrax* has a gross tonnage of 543 and was completed in 1994 in Norway by Sigbjørn Iversen M/V A/S, Flekkefjord. She has a bollard pull of 62 tonnes ahead and 58 tonnes going astern and has a pair of Ulstein directional propellers mounted aft. In 2008 she was transferred to Bantry Bay in southern Ireland. She was on loan from Bantry Bay when noted at Swansea on 14 May 2014. The *Thrax* was sold by Østensjø in 2017 to Atlantic Towage and Marine Ltd and placed under the Irish flag as *Ocean Challenger*. She was still working at Bantry Bay in 2019.

(Mike Aldron)

The *Svitzer Brunel* is a visitor from Avonmouth and Portbury and is seen off Mumbles Head on 20 April 2009. The *Svitzer Brunel* was delivered to the Bristol fleet in September 2003 and was one of four similar tugs for Svitzer Marine Ltd. The others are *Svitzer Bristol*, *Svitzer Bidston* and *Svitzer Bootle*. She was launched as *Severngarth* by Astilleros Zamakona, Viscaya, in Spain, but completed as *Svitzer Brunel*. She features Z-Peller propulsion with two units powered by a pair of Niigata type 6L-26HLX diesels delivering 4087bhp. This gives her a speed of just over 12 knots and a bollard pull of 58.5 tonnes. The *Svitzer Brunel* is also a fire-fighting tug with a self-protection spray system for the superstructure. In early 2019 the *Svitzer Brunel* was based at Gravesend along with *Svitzer Bootle*.

(Danny Lynch)

The 29 January 2011 was a fine day in Swansea Bay but Met Office records show that it was also quite a cold one. The *Portgarth* has come down from Portbury to help out at Port Talbot and is attached to a bulk carrier over her bow. She is a standard Damen ASD Tug to design 3110 and was delivered in March 1995 to Cory Towage Ltd for use at Avonmouth and Portbury. Her hull was constructed by PO Sevmash Predpriyatiye, Severodvinsk, and launched on 3 November 1993. Severodvinsk is in the White Sea in northern Russia. She was then towed to the Netherlands and completed by Scheepswerf Damen BV at Gorinchem. The *Portgarth* has an overall length of 100 feet and a gross tonnage of 262. She is powered by two 9-cylinder Stork-Wärtsilä diesels of 4052bhp that give her a bollard pull of around 50 tonnes. She later passed to Wijsmuller in 2000 and then to Svitzer Marine Ltd and remained based in the upper Bristol Channel until she was sold in 2018. In 2019 she can be found at work at Poti Sea Port in the Black Sea, under the flag of Georgia and still sailing as *Portgarth*.

(Danny Lynch)

In 1996 Howard Smith Towage Ltd took delivery of three powerful tugs to Damen's ASD Tug 3211 design which would be based at Felixstowe and the Medway. The first of these was **Melton** in May 1996 followed by **Bentley** and **Lady Madeleine**, the latter going to the Medway fleet. Their hulls were completed in Poland by Stocznia Polnocna SA at Gdansk, and were towed to Damen's yard at Gorinchem to be completed. The **Melton** is powered by a pair of Ruston diesels with a combined output of 4896bhp, and these drive a pair of stern-mounted Aquamaster propulsion units resulting in a bollard pull of 60 tonnes when running ahead. Howard Smith was taken over by Adsteam (UK) Ltd in May 2001 who in turn passed to Svitzer Marine in 2007. The trio were subsequently renamed **Svitzer Melton**, **Svitzer Bentley** and **Svitzer Madeleine**. The **Svitzer Melton** was later based at Southampton until her move to the Swansea fleet in 2012. She was subsequently joined at Swansea by **Svitzer Bentley** and finally **Svitzer Madeleine** which had latterly been on the Humber. On 31 July 2019 **Svitzer Melton** is acting as stern tug on the Keynvor MorLift barge **Selina**, which was arriving at Swansea for drydocking.

(Mike Aldron)

We now look at tugs at Port Talbot. The three 1000ihp steam tugs *Canada*, *Formby* and *Gladstone* of 1951 signalled the start of the post-war fleet modernisation for Alexandra Towing. These fine-looking 237grt tugs were completed by Cochrane & Sons Ltd, Selby, and followed the design of some of the Empire-type tugs built during WWII. All three were initially based at Liverpool, but *Gladstone* moved to Southampton in 1952 followed in 1956 by *Canada*. The *Formby* was also based at the south coast port for a while. At the end of her Alexandra Towing days *Formby* was based at Swansea, but for less than two years. However,

she seems to have been well photographed during her time based at the Welsh port. This view of her at Port Talbot in April 1969 gives the reader and possibly tug modeller, a clear view of her bridge/wheelhouse, funnel and towing gear. When built she had a short mast aft of her funnel port and a port-side lifeboat which has now been replaced by two inflatable life rafts. The height of her funnel was reduced when her boiler was converted to burn oil. As mentioned on page 7, *Formby* was sold to Italian buyers later in 1969.

(*Danny Lynch*)

The motor tug **Margam** of 1953 was rarely photographed and is seen here at Port Talbot in March 1969. Alexandra Towing purchased her in 1966 from Tees Towing Co Ltd (William H Crosthwaite & Son), Middlesbrough. She was previously **Caedmon Cross** and was built by Scott & Sons (Bowling) Ltd on the Clyde. Her main engine was a 4-cylinder two-stroke Crossley of 750bhp and she was the first diesel tug for a British owner to have geared propulsion which consisted of a 2:1 ratio reverse reduction gearbox manufactured by Hindmarch Modern Wheel Drive Ltd. Such was her success that Tees Towing ordered two further very similar tugs. Her overall length of 86 feet meant that **Margam** was well suited to work at Port Talbot docks with its small lock. This dock was soon replaced by the new tidal harbour that took large ships requiring powerful tugs. Therefore, after just four years' service **Margam** was sold to Sleepdienst Willem Muller N.V. of Terneuzen in 1970 and renamed **Rilland**. She was fitted with an 8-cylinder Appingedammer Brons diesel in 1971 and given a smaller funnel. She was lost in the Bay of Biscay in 1989 when in service with J Koek of Dordrecht.

(Danny Lynch)

Alexandra Towing's first new motor tugs, **North Isle** and **North Loch** of 1959, were followed by a second pair also from the shipyard of W J Yarwood & Sons. These were destined for service at Swansea and Port Talbot and received local names despite being registered in Liverpool. They were delivered in July and October 1961 as **Gower** and **Talbot**, and each had a controllable-pitch propeller in a steerable Kort nozzle. The **Gower** had an overall length of 95 feet and was powered by an 8-cylinder Crossley Bros two-stroke diesel engine of 865bhp. Here she is towing the Norwegian ore/oil carrier **Varangnes** in the dock system at Port Talbot on 16 February 1969. At this time **Gower** tended to be kept at Port Talbot on a regular basis, but once the new tidal harbour opened in May 1970, the old docks were closed, and all tugs were based at Swansea. The **Gower** passed to Greek owners Koutalidis Panagiotis as **Kostas** in 1986, and was later sailing as **Faethon**. By 2010 she was at Volos being used as a source of spare parts.

(the late John Wiltshire)

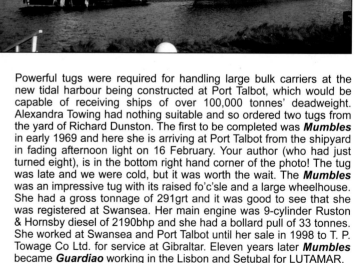

Powerful tugs were required for handling large bulk carriers at the new tidal harbour being constructed at Port Talbot, which would be capable of receiving ships of over 100,000 tonnes' deadweight. Alexandra Towing had nothing suitable and so ordered two tugs from the yard of Richard Dunston. The first to be completed was **Mumbles** in early 1969 and here she is arriving at Port Talbot from the shipyard in fading afternoon light on 16 February. Your author (who had just turned eight), is in the bottom right hand corner of the photo! The tug was late and we were cold, but it was worth the wait. The **Mumbles** was an impressive tug with its raised fo'c'sle and a large wheelhouse. She had a gross tonnage of 291grt and it was good to see that she was registered at Swansea. Her main engine was 9-cylinder Ruston & Hornsby diesel of 2190bhp and she had a bollard pull of 33 tonnes. She worked at Swansea and Port Talbot until her sale in 1998 to T. P. Towage Co Ltd. for service at Gibraltar. Eleven years later **Mumbles** became **Guardiao** working in the Lisbon and Setubal for LUTAMAR.

(the late John Wiltshire)

This lovely image of the *Canning* was taken at Port Talbot in March 1969 when the old docks were still quite active mainly with ore carriers for the nearby steel works. The *Canning* entered service at Liverpool in July 1954, and was the sister to *Wallasey* and *Waterloo*. She was completed for Alexandra Towing by Cochrane & Sons Ltd and had a triple expansion steam engine of 825ihp. The name *Canning* relates to a small area in Liverpool after which one of the docks is named. It had been carried by two previous Alexandra Towing steam tugs. The tug *Canning* transferred to Swansea in 1965 and put in a further ten years at the port. When she retired in 1975 the use of steam tugs for ship handling at ports and harbours in the UK had virtually come to an end. The only exception was Falmouth where steam tugs continued to work until 1983. In 2019 *Canning* can be found as an exhibit at the National Waterfront Museum in Swansea.

(the late Des Harris)

The size of vessels able to enter the original enclosed docks at Port Talbot was limited by the small lock, and so in 1966 a start was made on the construction of a deep-water tidal harbour. Westminster Dredging were involved in its construction and deployed the small tug *Beaver Crest* for a while. She was completed in 1957 by Tans Metaal Maatschappij NV, Krimpen aan den Ijssel as *Pegasus* for Tans Metaalconstructie NV, but had passed to Westminster Dredging Co Ltd, London by the end of that year. Renamed *Beaver Crest*, she spent four years working in eastern Canada returning to the UK in 1962. In 1966 her Dutch-built diesel engine was replaced by a more powerful Ruston & Hornsby unit of 495bhp. This view of her at Port Talbot was taken on 21 August 1968. The new harbour received its first ship in March 1970 and was officially opened by Her Majesty the Queen on 12 May 1970, and was the largest dry-bulk cargo facility in the UK. The *Beaver Crest* continued to work for Westminster Dredging until 1984 when she sank in the River Humber. She was later raised and scrapped.

(the late John Wiltshire)

The *Wallasey* was transferred to Swansea in 1988 from Liverpool principally for use at Port Talbot. She was a powerful tug that was technically a descendant of *Mumbles* and *Margam*, but without the raised fo'c'sle. She was built by Richard Dunston (Hessle) Ltd, Hessle and delivered to her owner Alexandra Towing Co Ltd in December 1977. She had a sistership, *Sun London*, which was completed for service on the Thames. The *Wallasey* was powered by a 12-cylinder vee-type Ruston diesel engine that delivered 2640bhp. This gave her a bollard pull of 45 tonnes and speed of 12 knots. Propulsion was by way of a controllable-pitch propeller rotating in a steerable Kort nozzle. Here she is seen entering the tidal harbour at Port Talbot on 15 April 1991 to assist with the sailing of the bulk carrier *Ocean Commander*. The *Wallasey* passed to Howard Smith Towage in 1993 when they acquired the business of Alexandra Towing and was occasionally used for coastal towing. She remained at Swansea until 1996 when she was sold to Greek owners at Piraeus. Renamed *Karapiperis 14* she was still in service in 2018 with Stavros Karapiperis.

(Andrew Wiltshire)

This tug was most probably at Port Talbot to assist with the movement of contractor's barges or pontoons that had been used in the construction of the new harbour and berths that had opened a few months earlier. The **Michel Petersen** was photographed on 12 October 1970 and was a West German tug of 195 gross tons that was owned and operated by Petersen & Alpers of Hamburg. She featured diesel electric propulsion and was completed in November 1964 by Schiffswerft Johann Oelkers KG, Hamburg. Her machinery consisted of two 8-cylinder MAN diesels of 2140bhp, each driving a generator. These supplied power to a pair of 1070shp electric motors which were geared to a single propeller shaft.

Her single screw rotated in a Kort nozzle and **Michel Petersen** had a bollard pull of 25 tonnes. She later sailed under the British flag as in 1985 she passed to Klyne-Winney Tugs Ltd of Lowestoft who by 1987 had become Klyne Tugs (Lowestoft) Ltd. In 1991 she was sold to Uruguayan owner Remolcadores y Lanchas SA, but sank in April 2003 after colliding with a container ship in Montevideo harbour. She was raised but declared a total loss. In 2007 she passed to an Italian owner for rebuilding into a yacht at Escobar, but in 2011 work had yet to start on this project.

(the late John Wiltshire)

The **Ryan** was one of the pair of terminal tugs that West Coast Towing purchased from South African Transport Services in 1994. The **Ryan** was completed in November 1977 by Dorman Long VanderBijl Corp Ltd, Durban, as **C M Hoffe**, and delivered to her owner Government of the Republic of South Africa (Railways & Harbour Administration) for service at Richards Bay coal exporting port. With a gross tonnage of 528 she was a large twin-screw vessel with a fire-fighting capability. A bollard pull of 53 tonnes was attainable and her engines comprised a pair of 16-cylinder Mirrlees-Blackstone diesels with a total output of 4000bhp. This superb profile of the **Ryan** was recorded in Swansea Bay on 14 April 1995, with the steel works complex at Port Talbot in the distance. The tug has an overall length of nearly 138 feet and this view gives the reader a clear view of her ample accommodation and prominent funnel. The **Ryan** and her sister **Faris** were highly regarded as very good sea boats, especially when working in a heavy swell out in Swansea Bay. West Coast Towing's Swansea operation passed to Wijsmuller Marine in May 2001 which in turn was acquired by Svitzer (A P Møller) in October 2001. Svitzer Port Talbot Ltd was formed in 2002 comprising four tugs, which included both **Ryan** and **Faris**.

(Nigel Jones)

The *Faris* was identical to *Ryan* in most respects and was completed at the same shipyard but was a little newer being delivered to her owner in March 1979 as *F H Boltman*. She was also based at Richards Bay terminal near Durban. When acquired by West Coast Towing in January 1994, both tugs were sailed to the UK. They covered the 897 miles from Richards Bay to Cape Town arriving on 2 February to take on bunkers. They then continued on 3 February arriving at Las Palmas on 21 February, 4455 miles and 18½ days later. With fresh bunkers on board both tugs sailed on 24 February bound for Newport, where they arrived on 3 March having covered a further 1530 miles. This view of *Faris* was taken in 2000 when she was in the colourful livery of her new owner Wijsmuller Marine. Both *Faris* and *Ryan* remained at Swansea and Port Talbot until 2005 by which time they were in Svitzer ownership. They were then sold to Al Jazeera Shipping of Bahrain for use on a tug/barge contract in the Arabian Gulf. They were renamed *Atlas* and *Hercules* respectively under the flag of Bahrain.

(Danny Lynch)

The *Westgarth* of 1983 was the third tug to carry this name but was quite different from the earlier examples. She was built in Japan by Hanazaki Zosensho K.K., Yokosuka and completed as *Yashima* for Daito Unyu K.K., Tokyo. In 1992 she was purchased by Cory Towage Ltd, renamed *Westgarth*, and put to work at Avonmouth and Portbury alongside the similar but somewhat smaller *Avongarth*. The *Westgarth* was powered by a pair of 6-cylinder Niigata diesels developing a total of 3000bhp which drove a pair of Niigata Z-peller tug propulsion units.

This gave her bollard pull of 40 tonnes and speed of 11 knots. Cory were taken over by Wijsmuller Marine Ltd in 2000, which in turn passed to Svitzer Marine Ltd in 2001, and *Westgarth* remained at Portbury throughout. In this view she has sailed down to Port Talbot to help out, and is seen on a bitterly cold 21 December 2010. The *Westgarth* was sold by Svitzer in 2016, and by 2018 was working at the Black Sea port of Yuzhnyy in the Ukraine. She transferred to the Liberian flag but with no change of name.

(Danny Lynch)

In 1984 the Dover Harbour Board replaced its two twin-screw motor tugs the *Diligent* and *Dominant* with a pair of Voith Schneider tractor tugs named *Deft* and *Dextrous*. These were in turn replaced in 2000 with a pair of powerful stern-drive tugs. The *Deft* and *Dextrous* were soon purchased by Howard Smith Towage Ltd to upgrade their fleet at Gravesend and were renamed *Shorne* and *Cobham* respectively. They passed to Adsteam Towage Ltd in 2001, and to Svitzer Tugs Ltd in 2007. At this point they transferred to Humber Tugs Ltd, a subsidiary of Svitzer, and became *HT Scimitar* and *HT Cutlass* respectively. By 2009 the pair were based in the upper Bristol Channel fleet, but often helped out at Port Talbot. The *HT Scimitar* is seen at Port Talbot on 18 July 2009, pushing-up to exactly the correct spot as indicated by the arrow on the bulk carrier's hull. In 2013 the *HT Scimitar* and *HT Cutlass* were on the move again, but to South America this time. They took up service in Venezuela with Svitzer (Americas) Ltd.

(Danny Lynch)

West Coast Towing (UK) Ltd was awarded the contract to provide towage at Port Talbot tidal harbour in 1994 and from 1996 larger ships visited the port thanks to a major dredging project, and thus there was a requirement for extra larger, more powerful tugs. The former *Kelty* of Forth Tugs Ltd, Grangemouth, was acquired in 1997 and renamed *Shireen S*. She was one of the four tugs that were based at the Hound Point terminal on the Firth of Forth, but had become redundant due to the loss of the contract. The *Kelty* was a powerful single-screw tug with a bollard pull of 36 tonnes that had been completed by Richards (Shipbuilders) Ltd, Lowestoft, in 1976. When the West Coast Towing operation at Swansea passed to Wijsmuller Marine Ltd in May 2001, a new tug unit was set up as Wijsmuller Port Talbot Ltd. This proved to be shortlived as Svitzer Marine Ltd took over Wijsmuller in 2001 and the livery changed once again. The *Shireen S* now in mainly Svitzer colours, is seen at Port Talbot on 18 August 2002. She was sold in 2005 to Saga Shipping & Trading of Oslo, without a change of name, and by 2007 was sailing under Panamanian registry. In 2013 she became *W Power* under Moldovan registry, and in 2016 was working in the eastern Mediterranean.

(Danny Lynch)

We now move east to Barry where the operation of steam tugs came to an end in 1966 with the departure of the relatively youthful tug *Westgarth* of 1954. Five modern motor tugs had been delivered to R & J H Rea at Cardiff and Barry in the years 1965/66, all constructed by Richards (Shipbuilders) Ltd of Lowestoft. The *Uskgarth* was delivered to South Wales in March 1966, and along with *Bargarth* would be based at Barry for a good number of years. In the late 1960s three tugs were often stationed at Barry with four being kept at Cardiff, but they regularly moved between ports when required. As shipping movements at Barry began to decline in the 1970s, the tug allocation was reduced to just *Uskgarth* and *Bargarth*. This view of *Uskgarth* was taken off Barry on 14 November 1971 when she was in the colours of Cory Ship Towage. Clearly visible in this view is the spar attached to her main mast, which instantly distinguished her from her sisters. By the mid-1980s *Uskgarth* was usually based at Cardiff from where she could easily be deployed to Newport, Barry or even Avonmouth.

(Nigel Jones)

On 25 January 1975 the **Bargarth** heads back to Barry in a lively sea and dramatic lighting. The photographer was no doubt pleased with this result, which is not what you expect in the UK on the average January afternoon. It must be said that in this lighting, the Cory livery seems to look quite effective on the **Bargarth**. The **Bargarth** entered service in July 1966 with R & J H Rea Ltd, Cardiff, passing to Cory Ship Towage with the takeover of Rea in 1970. She was powered by an 8-cylinder Blackstone diesel of 860bhp which drove a fixed-pitch propeller rotating in a steerable Kort nozzle. Note the radar antenna on her mast. The **Bargarth** had radar from new, whereas her sisters were not equipped with this navigational aid until later in their lives. Having left the Bristol Channel in 2002, **Bargarth** had a number of subsequent owners, and was noted by your author at Falmouth in April 2017 working for Keynvor MorLift Ltd of Appledore as **Tennaherdhya**. However, by late 2017 she had moved to a new base on the Thames estuary as **TTMS Viking** for TTM Services (UK) Ltd.

(Nigel Jones)

The small tug **Peter Leigh** was a welcome visitor to Barry from the Bristol area when photographed in the outer harbour on 8 August 1976. She was most probably heading back to Avonmouth, having delivered one or two barges laden with grain for the Rank Hovis flour mills in No.2 Dock. The **Peter Leigh** had been owned by F A Ashmead & Son Ltd of Bristol since 1970 and had previously sailed as **John King** for C J King & Sons Ltd, Bristol. She was Bristol-built having been completed in February 1936 by Charles Hill & Sons Ltd, and was a relatively early motor tug that was originally powered by a 300bhp Petter diesel. In 1962 this was removed and replaced by a slightly more powerful Lister-Blackstone diesel of 337bhp. The **Peter Leigh** was sold by Ashmead in 1976, becoming **Pride** in 1978 for Bristol Commercial Ships Ltd. In 1992 she was renamed **Durdham** and remained in the Bristol/upper Severn estuary area. In 1994 she was purchased by the Bristol Industrial Museum for preservation, and regained her original name **John King** two years later. She was then restored at her new base in the City Docks, and since 2000 has been a working exhibit at the museum.

(Nigel Jones)

In 1985 Associated British Ports moved the Geest banana terminal to a berth in the No. 3 dock. This required the installation of dockside cranes and so it was decided to relocate three from Cardiff to Barry. A large floating crane **Hebe I** was to be used to move each crane individually around the coast to Barry. The operation was carried out using the German tug **Axel**. The **Axel** was a large harbour/coastal towing tug built in 1964 for use at Hamburg in the fleet of Bugsier Reederei- und Bergungs AG. Completed as **Bugsier 26** she and her sistership **Bugsier 27** were constructed at the yard of Schichau-Unterweser, Bremerhaven. She was powered by a 6-cylinder Deutz diesel of 1600bhp and had a bollard pull of 27 tonnes. In 1977 **Bugsier 26** was sold to J Johanssen & Sohn, Lübeck, who rebuilt her and renamed her **Axel**. This image was taken at Barry on the evening of 2 July 1985. She passed to Danish owner Nils Hojlund Hansen, Svendborg, in 1988 as **Baltic Stevns** and by 2002 was based in the UK with Eimon Guerrini (Teico Marine Solutions Ltd), Essex. Now named **Baltic Warrior** it was intended that she would be used for film and TV projects. She is believed to be still in existence.

(Andrew Wiltshire)

The **Chimera** is by far the oldest tug to appear in this book having been constructed as long ago as 1880. What is even more remarkable is that as I write this in 2019, she is still at work. She has without doubt been rebuilt, updated and modified on a number of occasions over the last 139 years, but I think we can safely say that her hull is probably more or less original. She was completed in Sweden in 1880 by Kockums Mek. Verkstads A/B, Malmø, as the steam tug **Skjelsvik** for an unknown Swedish owner. She had an overall length of about 64 feet and her machinery comprised a 2-cylinder compound steam engine of 110ihp. Her history between 1880 and 1931 is not really known except that she was renamed **Vildanden** at some point, and later **Munkholmen**. In 1931 she passed to Norwegian owner Dyre Halse of Trondheim and was renamed **Cito**. She was later to receive a diesel engine and was renamed **Cito I**. By 1982 she was with Handelsfinans A/S, Stavanger, and in 1991 came to the UK for service with Manor Marine Ltd, Portland, as **Chimera**. She was still with Manor Marine in 2019 who it appears has spent time and money updating her.

(Paul Andow)

Ship handling at Cardiff and Barry was revolutionised in 1979 when Cory Ship Towage took delivery of their new Voith-Schneider tractor tugs *Holmgarth* and *Hallgarth*. Each had a pair of forward-mounted Voith Schneider propulsion units and they were the first tugs of this type to enter service in the Bristol Channel. The *Holmgarth* was delivered on 2 May by Scott & Sons (Bowling) Ltd. The *Holmgarth* was powered by a pair of Ruston 6RK3CM diesels with a combined output of 2190bhp. This gave her a bollard pull of 23½ tonnes and a speed of 11 knots. This view of her was taken in No.2 Dock at Barry on 19 June 1982. She was normally kept at Cardiff, but regularly visited Barry and Newport with the odd trip over to Avonmouth to help out. The *Holmgarth* spent a period at Liverpool in the 1990s, but returned to the Bristol Channel, working briefly at Swansea in 1998/99. She worked in these waters until 2008, latterly with Wijsmuller and then Svitzer Marine, and in 2019 was sailing as *Morgawr* for Fowey Harbour Commissioners.

(Andrew Wiltshire)

On 25 July 1990 the attractive German-built motor tug *Towing Wizard* is seen approaching the outer harbour at Barry. She was at this time involved attending the barge *Jimmy Mac*. This 137grt tug was completed in 1955 by Mützelfeldtwerft at Cuxhaven as *Quaysider* for Lawson-Batey Tugs Ltd, Newcastle. She was 97 feet long and was powered by an 8-cylinder 1200bhp Deutz diesel. She was based on the River Tyne for 29 years before being sold to TSA Tugs Ltd, Leigh-on-Sea, Essex, in 1984. Renamed *Towing Wizard* she became a familiar sight around the UK. In 1994 she passed to Medmarine Services SA (Seabulk Shipping SA). She became *Tora* under the Panama flag, and was put to work in Greek waters. By now looking rather shabby, in 2001 she became *Nafpigia Panagiotaki* in the ownership of Michael Xiradakis, Piraeus. It is thought that she was broken up in about 2005.

(Nigel Jones)

The twin-screw motor tug *Goliath* is seen in the cut at Barry on 28 May 1989 on her way to collect a barge from No.2 Dock. She was engaged on an outfall contract off Barry. She was now 33 years old and had started life in 1956 as *M.S.C. Scimitar* working for the Manchester Ship Canal Company as a ship handling tug on the canal. She was one of a class of four similar tugs constructed by P K Harris & Sons Ltd, Appledore, with a gross tonnage of 147 and an overall length of 95 feet. She featured a hydroconic hull and was powered by a pair of Ruston & Hornsby diesels with a combined output of 1290bhp. She was withdrawn from service on the Manchester Ship Canal and laid up

for some time before being sold to Spithead Trading Co Ltd in 1987. The intention was to rename her *Vulkan*, but this was changed to *Goliath* when she entered service under the flag of Saint Vincent and the Grenadines. In 2006 she passed to Griffin Towage (Jon Evelegh) Ltd which has its registered office in Unit 9, Luccombe Business Park, Milton Abbas, Blandford Forum. The operating base is Sydenham Wharf, Poole. The *Goliath* was transferred to the UK flag, registered at London and was still in service with this owner in 2019.

(the late John Wiltshire)

The **Butegarth** was the first of the four new motor tugs delivered to R & J H Rea Ltd in 1966. She arrived on 25 January 1966 from the shipyard of Richards (Shipbuilders) Ltd, Lowestoft, having been launched the previous October. These tugs had a gross tonnage of 161 and unlike the evaluation tug **Lowgarth** of 1965, they were powered by an 8-cylinder Blackstone diesel of 862bhp. The **Butegarth** had a bollard pull of 14 tonnes and a speed of 10 knots. Normally kept at Cardiff, she passed with the Rea business to Cory Ship Towage Ltd in 1970. She was transferred to Newport in 1979. This view of **Butegarth** was taken at Barry on 1 April 1986, and she was then in the new colours introduced in 1985 when her owner was restyled as Cory Towage Ltd. The **Butegarth** was the first of the four to be sold, passing to Arklow Shipping Ltd in 1989, and renamed **Avoca** in 1990. Later in 1990 she was sold to Fluvialsado Ltda, Setubal, Portugal as **Lutamar**. She was often to be found based at Lisbon, and at some point she was re-engined with a Lister-Blackstone diesel of 1306bhp giving her a revised bollard pull of 20 tonnes. The **Lutamar** was last noted by your author at Lisbon in 2014.

(the late John Wiltshire)

The **Emsgarth** is about to pass through the breakwaters at Barry outer harbour on 16 June 1996, and will most probably head up channel to Cardiff or Newport. She is in the attractive livery introduced from 1985 when Cory Ship Towage restyled their business to Cory Towage Ltd. Initially the deckhouse and engine room casing were brown but this was later changed to a buff colour. The **Emsgarth** was the second former German tug that Cory added to their Newport fleet in the mid-1980s. She was completed in March 1975 by Cassens Werftunion GmbH & Co, Emden, as **Juist** for Ems Schlepper AG, Emden. She was broadly similar to their **Norderney** of 1972 which became Cory's **Gwentgarth** in 1983 (see front cover). The **Juist** joined the Cory fleet in 1984 as **Emsgarth** and replaced the **Dalegarth** of 1960. She was a popular tug as she was compact and powerful with a bollard pull of 26 tonnes and a bow thruster for extra manoeuvrability. She passed to Wijsmuller Marine Ltd on 29 February 2000 and was placed under Honduras registry. The **Emsgarth** continued to serve south-east Wales, latterly with Svitzer Marine until her sale in 2005 to Moroccan interests. She was still at work in 2018 as **Iltizam** for Dragage des Ports SA (DRAPOR), Casablanca.

(Nigel Jones)

In this view in the outer harbour at Barry on 31 October 2007, the ASD tug **Flying Spindrift** is attached to the stern of the chemical tanker **Cape Elwood**. She is a powerful tug of 3100bhp that was completed in early 1986 by Richard Dunston (Hessle) Ltd for Clyde Shipping Co Ltd, Glasgow, the company's last new tug. She features a pair of Aquamaster propulsion units driven by 6-cylinder Ruston diesel engines. In 1994 she was transferred to the Tyne to work for associated tug fleet Lawson-Batey Tugs Ltd, Newcastle. The Clyde Shipping operation was taken over by Cory Towage Ltd in May 1995 and the **Flying Spindrift** gained Cory colours. She then passed through Wijsmuller Marine into Svitzer Marine ownership and continued to work on the Tyne until transferred to the south-east Wales fleet. In 2009 she passed into Svitzer's Felixarc Marine subsidiary, and in 2012 was sold to Norwegian owner Farsund Fortøjningsselskap A/S (A Nielsen), Farsund. She was placed under the flag of St Vincent and the Grenadines as **FFS Atlas**, and was still in service in 2019.

(Paul Andow)

Barry had its fair share of visiting tugs over the years and these included a number of ocean-going vessels. It is probably safe to say that the largest example was **Rotterdam** which was in Barry for repairs in 2007. She is seen in No.2 dock on 25 September and may have been in port for two to three weeks. She was by now quite an elderly tug having been completed in April 1975 as **Smit Rotterdam** for Smit Internationale Zeesleep- en Bergingsbedrijf, Rotterdam. She was followed by her sistership **Smit London** and the pair were completed at the shipyard of Scheepswerf & Machinefabriek De Merwede v/h van Vliet & Co, Hardinxveld. The **Smit Rotterdam** was a twin-screw tug with a gross tonnage of 2273, an overall length of 245 feet and a breadth of 51 feet. Her main engines were a pair of 9-cylinder Stork-Werkspoor diesels with a total output of 13500bhp. Her bollard pull was 180 tonnes and she had a speed of 13 knots. The **Smit Rotterdam** was naturally capable of extensive salvage work and was fitted for fire-fighting. She moved about extensively within the Smit group between 1986 and 2005, and in 2006 became part of Wijsmuller and was managed by Smitwijs Towage BV. In 2007 management changed to Svitzer Ocean Towage and she was renamed **Rotterdam** as seen here. In 2014 she passed to Pakistani breakers as **Global Destiny**.

(Paul Andow)

In 2019 the SMS Towage fleet comprised eighteen ASD-type tugs, with three usually based in the upper Bristol Channel. However back in 2012, the year in which SMS established their operation in south-east Wales, the fleet included two Voith Schneider tractor tugs. The **Roman** was of German origin, having been completed by Detlef Hegemann Rolandwerft GmbH, Bremen, in December 1983, as **Midgard III** for Stinnes Aktiengesellschaft, Nordenham. She had twin propulsion units and a bollard pull 25 tonnes. She was fitted for fire-fighting and her hull was constructed to navigate in ice. Her owner was later given as Midgard Deutsche Seeverkehrs AG, Nordenham, and in 2004 she passed to Unterweser Reederei AG, Bremen as **Brake**. She was then transferred to associated company Lütgens & Reimers at Hamburg in 2012, and was placed on charter to SMS Towage Ltd as **Roman**. This view of her was taken on 30 March 2012, and **Roman** later appeared with an orange hull. She had left the Bristol Channel by 2016 and had returned to Unterweser Reederei AG (URAG) in Germany. By 2019 she was sailing as **VB Brake**, which reflects that Unterweser is part of the Spanish group Boluda Corporación Maritima.

(Paul Andow)

In addition to harbour towage West Coast Towing became involved in coastal and deep sea towing, and as a result, acquired an interesting selection of vessels in the 1990s to undertake this work. One such tug was *Sir Michael* which is seen on arrival at Barry on 18 July 1997. She had brought the dredger *Lady of Chichester* from the south coast to be laid up in Barry. The *Sir Michael* had been purchased by Yale Invest & Finance SA in 1995 and was managed by West Coast Towing Offshore Ltd, Swansea. She sailed under Honduran registry, which is how we see her here. She was completed in Germany in June 1973 as *Bever* by D W Kremer Sohn, Elmshorn. She and her sister *Bison* entered

service with Norwegian owner Bukser Bjergningsselkapet, Oslo. She was a twin-screw tug with a bollard pull of 60 tonnes and was fitted for fire-fighting and pollution control. In 1981 she was sold to Pacific Offshore as *Cherdas* under the Panamanian flag. Then from 1985 she sailed as *Abu Samir* for BBT International Inc. under Honduran registry until joining the West Coast Towing fleet in 1995. She was under arrest from 2003 until at least 2007, and at some point thought to be around 2011 she was sold. She retained her name *Sir Michael* with a number of owners until 2013, when she was renamed *Kunduz* and placed under Panamanian registry.

(Nigel Jones)

The tug **MTS Vengeance** is operated by MTS Group Ltd (Marine & Towage Services) based at Brixham, Devon. Their vessels provide a range of support including towing, salvage and civil engineering work. The **MTS Vengeance** was at Barry on 4 March 2013 and had accompanied the non-propelled cargo barge **Terra Marique**. The **MTS Vengeance** had a gross tonnage of 156 and was powered by two Ruston diesels delivering 1900bhp and a bollard pull of 28 tonnes. The tug had previously sailed for Fairplay of Hamburg as **Fairplay X**

from 2000 until 2007 and was based at Rotterdam. However, she was originally a British tug having been completed in 1987 by Cochrane Shipbuilders Ltd, Goole, as **Lady Sybil** for Humber Tugs Ltd. She was notably the last ship built at Cochrane's Goole yard. She was one of a group of four identical twin-screw tugs for use at Hull, the other three being constructed at Selby. She was still in use in 2019.

(Paul Andow)

The colourful livery of R & J H Rea Ltd suited most motor tugs and the four vessels from Richards (Shipbuilders) Ltd in 1966 were no exception. The Cory Ship Towage livery that followed from 16 July 1970 whilst bold, lacked the same character. The **Danegarth** is noted at Cardiff on 4 May 1969 approaching the entrance to the main lock. She was delivered to Rea in April 1966 and had a gross tonnage of 161 and an overall length of 95 feet. A single arm davit was used for the lifeboat in place of traditional davits. The **Danegarth** remained a Cardiff-based tug until 1979 when the arrival of the two new tractor tugs saw her transfer to Newport along with **Butegarth**. She was the second of the quartet to be sold, departing Newport in 1992 for Greek waters. Here the former **Danegarth** settled down at the port of Heraklion on the island of Crete. Having been renamed **Linoperamata** by 1993, she could still be found working for Linoperamata Shipping Company in 2019.

(the late John Wiltshire)

R & J H Rea Ltd operated an interesting pair of 500bhp Dutch-built motor tugs in the Bristol Channel. They were completed in 1958 by Scheepswerf P. de Vries-Lentsch, Alphen a/d Rijn, for Overseas Towage & Salvage Co Ltd's ship towage subsidiary Milford Haven Tug Services Ltd as the *Cleddia* and *Neylandia*. They passed to Rea in 1961 and were registered at Bristol as *Falgarth* and *Tregarth* respectively. The *Tregarth* soon moved to the new Rea operation at Cardiff in 1962, and is seen here at anchor off Penarth. By 1967, and with all the steam tugs at Cardiff and Barry having been replaced, the *Tregarth* remained at Cardiff as the spare tug. She was sold in 1970 just prior to the Cory takeover and sailed for a new life in Trinidad as *GW180* for Wimpey Marine Ltd, Great Yarmouth. By 1975 she was still based in Trinidad as *MABCO 180* for Malcolm A Browne & Co, San Fernando, and by 1977 was reported as having sunk. However, in 1983, she was reported to be owned by Swan Hunter (Trinidad) Ltd, Chaguaramas, as *Tug 180*.

(the late Des Harris)

The West German tug *Fairplay XI* made at least two visits to Cardiff in the late 1960s. Probably the most memorable was in March 1968 when she arrived to tow the paddle steamer *Bristol Queen* away to Willebroek in Belgium for breaking up. This interesting view was taken on 5 October 1967 in the Roath Basin at Cardiff. It shows *Fairplay XI* in the company of Rea's tugs *Butegarth*, *Lowgarth* and *Plumgarth*. The local British Transport Docks Board dredging fleet had been upgraded with modern vessels, and the bucket dredger *Taff* (of 1946) had been withdrawn from service. Consequently, some of the steam hopper barges that worked with the *Taff* were now redundant, and one of these, *G.W.R. No.1* (built 1933), is seen here. She was towed away for scrap by *Fairplay XI* which had been built at Emden in 1963 as *Aro* for Reederei Adolf A Ronnebaum, Emden. The following year she passed to Fairplay of Hamburg as *Fairplay XI* but sank in January 1966 after a collision. She was raised and repaired and continued to work for Fairplay until 1990, when she was sold to Dutch owners.

(the late John Wiltshire)

During the winter of 1968 and into the spring of 1969 a major civil engineering project was underway on the Cardiff foreshore. It involved the construction of a new pumping station adjacent to Rover Way, and the laying of a new sewage pipeline out into the Bristol Channel. A number of tugs were periodically engaged on this project and one of them was the Dutch-flagged *Eos*. She was built and launched at the yard of Gebr. Hakvoort, Urk, in late 1966, but completed in 1967 by Egmond & van der Schee Machfbk at IJmuiden for service with J & S Engelsman of Badhoevedorp near Amsterdam. The *Eos* was a tug of 92grt powered by a 6-cylinder Mak diesel of 1200bhp that gave her an impressive bollard pull of 15 tonnes. Here she is seen returning to Cardiff docks during the late morning of 22 March 1969. Between 1977 and 2006, the *Eos* worked under the Dutch flag for a number of different owners and gained a new wheelhouse at some point. In 2006 she was renamed *St. Gabriel* upon her sale to the Polidano Group at Valletta, a civil engineering contractor. She was still working around Malta in May 2018, and was kept in very good condition.

(the late John Wiltshire)

The small single-screw tug **Red Branch** is seen at Cardiff at high tide on an evening in August 1968. She had been working on an outfall to the east of the port. The history of this tug is a little patchy. We know that she was built in 1927 at Zaltbommel in the Netherlands as **Bessey**, most probably as a motor tug. We do not know which shipyard or for whom she was completed. She passed to the Government of Northern Ireland, Belfast, in 1930 and was renamed **Red Branch**. By this time, we know that she had a gross tonnage of 60, an overall length of 65 feet and a breadth of 16 feet. Her diesel engine had an output of 120bhp. At some point in the 1960s she was sold to a UK owner and by the late 1960s was working for Bernard Williams & Co Ltd, Swansea. She was sold to T W Ward Ltd at Briton Ferry for scrap and arrived at their yard on 23 October 1973.

(the late Les Ring)

An interesting visitor to Cardiff from the Bristol side of the channel on 6 April 1970 was the small tug **Ernest Brown**. She has a couple of barges in tow which had delivered grain to Spillers mill in the Roath dock. The **Ernest Brown** dated from 1944 and was a TID-type steam tug. The TID class of tug was constructed during the latter part of WWII for the Ministry of War Transport. The **Ernest Brown** was completed by Richard Dunston Ltd at Thorne as **TID 95**, passing to T R Brown & Sons at Bristol in 1946. She was an oil-fired steam tug and her open wheelhouse was soon enclosed by Browns. The **Ernest Brown** was Brown's main channel tug, often crossing over to south-east Wales with grain barges. Following boiler problems her steam engine was removed in 1964 and replaced by a 295bhp Ruston & Hornsby diesel. Her wheelhouse was enlarged and a small funnel replaced her distinctive tall stack. In 1981 **Ernest Brown** sank at her moorings in Avonmouth docks, but was soon raised, repaired and sold. She ended her days in Brittany, but by 2004 was lying out of use. She was broken up on the quayside at Brest.

(the late John Wiltshire)

The **Pengarth** was an Avonmouth-based tug that made frequent visits to Cardiff to provide cover for an absent or unavailable local tug. She and her sister tug **Polgarth** were completed in 1962 at Bristol by Charles Hill & Sons Ltd for R & J H Rea Ltd. They had a gross tonnage of 160, and a 1080bhp Ruston and Hornsby diesel gave them a bollard pull of 14½ tonnes. This shot of the **Pengarth** in Rea colours was taken in the late afternoon sun of 22 May 1970. On 16 July 1970 the activities of R & J H Rea Ltd passed to Cory Ship Towage, whose livery then rapidly appeared across the fleet. The **Pengarth** remained at Avonmouth until 1991, when she was sold to Peninsular Shipping Co Ltd (MacGinnity & Wiltshire), Totnes, who immediately resold her to Captain R J Harvey of Grimsby. In 1992 she passed to Tyne Towage Ltd, South Shields, and continued to sail as **Pengarth**. By 1997 she had been sold to Togo Oil and Marine, Lomé, and sailed to West Africa as **Vigilant**. She is thought to be no longer in existence.

(the late John Wiltshire)

The family business of T R Brown & Sons was operating a number of small tugs in the Bristol area by the 1890s. They were mainly engaged on barge towing duties with some occasional salvage work. In 1965 the company was looking to replace the elderly tug *Medway* of 1906, the last steam tug in the fleet. The conversion of the *Ernest Brown* to motor had been a success, but *Medway* was considered too old for this. Consequently, a modern motor tug was sought and the Dutch-built *Niger* was purchased from de Ruiter & van de Wiel of Sliedrecht in June 1965. She was a small vessel of only 30 tons gross and with an overall length of 51 feet. She was completed by J van der Giessen, Sliedrecht, in November 1964, and was powered by an 8-cylinder MWM diesel of 232bhp. She entered service as *Medway*, the former *Medway* having been sent for scrapping. She was the last tug to be purchased by T R Brown, and in this view is seen arriving at Cardiff on 11 July 1970 with a laden grain barge in tow. This type of work was in rapid decline by the 1970s in the Bristol Channel and had ceased by 1980. The *Medway* went to work in Scotland and by 1991 was sailing as *Boojum Bay* for Clyde Marine Services Ltd, Greenock.

(the late John Wiltshire)

The Gulf Oil Corporation was granted permission by the Irish Government to construct a landscaped crude oil storage facility at Whiddy Island in Bantry Bay in County Cork. Crude oil would arrive in very large crude carriers (VLCCs), and eventually be transhipped in smaller tankers to oil refineries across Europe. Four powerful fire-fighting tugs would be needed, and the contract was awarded to R & J H Rea Ltd. Rea would manage the tugs on behalf of the Bantry Bay Towing Co Ltd. Two of the tugs (*Dingle Bay* and *Tralee Bay*) were built by Richard Dunston at Hessle, while the other pair (*Bantry Bay* and *Brandon Bay*) were completed at Beverley by Charles D Holmes & Co Ltd. The *Brandon Bay* was the last of the four to be handed over and is seen at Cardiff in August 1968 on a courtesy visit as part of her delivery trip. She has a gross tonnage of 299 and a 37½ ton bollard pull was obtained from her 2520bhp Mirrlees National diesel engine. When the tanker *Betelguese* exploded at the Whiddy Island terminal on 8 January 1979, the facility was badly damaged and was subsequently closed down by Gulf Oil. The four tugs were all transferred to Irish Tugs Ltd in 1979 and laid up by 1981. The *Brandon Bay* passed to Cory Towage Ltd and operated on the Clyde from 1985. She was eventually sold out of the Cory group in 1999 and passed to Togo Oil & Marine in 2005 as *Vigilant*.

(Danny Lynch)

On 1 August 1970 the British Transport Docks Board closed the port of Newport to undertake repairs to the outer cill in the lock. Shipping was diverted elsewhere and the two remaining Cory tugs were transferred to Cardiff. The Docks Board's own tugs remained in the port. Newport docks re-opened on 4 December 1970. On 7 August 1970 *Duncurlew* is waiting at the entrance to the lock at Cardiff. This former Newport Screw Towing tug is now wearing the funnel colours of her new owner Cory Ship Towage, but she would have to wait until the following year to receive her new name *Westgarth*. The *Duncurlew* dates from 1962 and was built on Humberside by Richard Dunston (Hessle) Ltd together with her sister ship *Dunsnipe*. They were the most powerful tugs in the Bristol Channel at the time with a brake horse power of 1260, and each operated with a crew of five comprising master, mate, engineer and two deck boys. It should be noted that *Duncurlew* is without a lifeboat, which was still absent in 1976.

(Nigel Jones)

The Dutch ocean-going salvage tug *Orinoco* makes a fine sight as she sails from Cardiff on 22 March 1972. Whilst the port was host to quite a number of visiting tugs over the years, Smit International's *Orinoco* must rank as one of the finest tugs to call. She was in port with a barge on which a much smaller tug was sitting, on its way to a new home. We are not quite sure why *Orinoco* and her tow were in Cardiff, but are fairly certain that the tug was already on the barge when she docked. The *Orinoco* was launched on 12 December 1963 at Kinderdijk in the Netherlands from the yard of J & K Smit's Scheepswerven. She was completed and delivered to L Smit & Co's Internationale Sleepdienst NV, Rotterdam, in May 1964. An impressive tug of 670grt and with an overall length of 175 feet, she was powered by a pair of Smit-MAN diesels of 2500bhp. These drove a single propeller giving her bollard pull 32 tonnes and speed of 15 knots. In early 1979 she was transferred to Smit International (South East Asia) Pte Ltd, initially under Singapore and later Bahamas registry. Smit sold her in 1984 to Indian interests, and by 1989 she was with Goa Towage & Salvage Pvt Ltd, Bombay. On 9 June 1998 during a cyclone, she sank off Sikka, Gujarat, whilst at anchor with the loss of all her crew.

(Nigel Jones)

On the previous day at Cardiff the photographer took this close up of the tug *Zweden* that was on the barge alongside *Orinoco*. Whilst we do not know why the tug and barge were in Cardiff, we do know a little about the *Zweden*. She was built in 1943 by Machinefabriek & Scheepswerf van P Smit Jr, Rotterdam, as *Linge* and delivered to Nederlandsche Stoomsleepdienst v/h van P Smit Jr of Rotterdam. She was a single-screw motor tug of 17 tons gross and powered by a 200bhp Brons diesel engine. In 1944 she saw service with Admiral in die Niederlanden Oberwerftsamt as *Narva*, and in 1945 returned to P Smit Jr, Rotterdam as *Haringvliet*. She was re-engined in 1960 with a new 6-cylinder Stork-Ricardo diesel of 300bhp and renamed *Zweden*. We then know that she was sold in late 1971 to Italian owner SAILEM of Palermo and eventually renamed *Stromboli*. In this view she is obviously being delivered to Italy.

(Nigel Jones)

A book on South Wales tugs would not be complete without an image of *Plumgarth*. Your author has fond memories of this tug, as it was the first tug he ever stepped aboard, when invited with his father to take a look over her at Barry in about 1968. In this view she is seen at Cardiff on 4 August 1973 in Cory Ship Towage colours. The *Plumgarth* and her sister *Avongarth* were delivered to R & J H Rea Ltd, in 1960 for service at Avonmouth. They had been completed by W J Yarwood and Sons and featured a Ruston & Hornsby engine of 870bhp. In 1962 *Plumgarth* was transferred to Cardiff and Barry when Rea set up a new tug base at these ports. The *Plumgarth* remained in south-east Wales until 1979 when she was transferred to Plymouth. She was sold to Greek owners in 1985 and renamed *Minotavros* for Minos Shipping Company. She was still in service at Heraklion in 2018.

(Nigel Jones)

The **Sea Alarm** was the last coal-fired steam tug at work in the Bristol Channel. She was a Warrior-class Empire-tug completed in 1941 by J Crown and Sons Ltd, Sunderland, as **Empire Ash**. She was initially owned by the Ministry of War Transport and based on the Clyde. In 1946 she passed to Clyde Shipping Co Ltd, Glasgow, as **Flying Fulmar**. Ten years later she was purchased by the Alarm Steam Tug Co Ltd, Bristol, and put to work as **Sea Alarm** in the Avonmouth-based fleet of C J King & Sons (Tugs) Ltd. She was withdrawn from service in 1972 and sold to T W Ward Ltd, Briton Ferry, in early 1973 for breaking up. However,

she was saved from this fate, and passed to the Welsh Industrial and Maritime Museum. This view of **Sea Alarm** was taken on 3 June 1974 at her permanent dry berth in the old Bute West Basin, which would be adjacent to the new Welsh Industrial and Maritime Museum. Here she lay until 1998, occasionally receiving a little cosmetic attention. In that fateful year she was declared no longer a worthy exhibit, and had become an obstacle in the redevelopment of the Cardiff Bay area. The museum was swept away, and **Sea Alarm** was broken up in situ.

(the late John Wiltshire)

It was a relatively common occurrence to see Avonmouth-based Cory tugs at Cardiff, as they were often sent over if Barry or Newport were unable to help out. However, it was most unusual to see examples from C J King's fleet at Cardiff, although in the 1960s and early 1970s they used to send their coal-fired steam tugs to Barry to replenish their bunkers. So far research has failed to throw any light on why the *Sea Bristolian* and *Sea Merrimac* are berthed in Cardiff's Queen Alexandra dock on 1 February 1973. This date rules out their involvement in towing the Royal Naval Reserve's former sloop HMS *Flying Fox* over from Bristol for scrapping, as it is about seven weeks too early. It is also too early to be attributed to the rescue of the steam tug *Sea Alarm* by the National Museum of Wales, from the hands of the shipbreaker T Ward at Briton Ferry. If any reader can help, then please get in touch. For the record *Sea Bristolian* was a motor tug of 1959 that began life with United Towing of Hull as *Foreman*. The *Sea Merrimac* was built for King's by Charles Hill at Bristol in 1964, and was one of three similar tugs in the fleet.

(the late John Wiltshire)

In April 1977 the British Transport Docks Board was able to sell off its towage operation at Newport to Cory Ship Towage. The deal included two out of the three tugs, and drew to a close the Board's involvement with ship towage across the UK, which dated back to when many ports were owned by the railway companies. The twin-screw tugs *Llanwern* and *St. Woolos* were renamed *Taffgarth* and *Wyegarth* respectively and continued to work at Newport gradually gaining the full Cory livery. The *Llanwern* differed from her sister as she featured diesel-electric propulsion of her two propeller shafts. Keen to dispose of these two tugs, the *Taffgarth* went on bareboat charter to the port authority at Londonderry in 1979. Here she is seen at Cardiff on 12 June 1979 about to sail for Londonderry. The photographer had brought her down from Newport and she was handed over to her new crew for the voyage to Northern Ireland. She was eventually purchased by the Londonderry Port and Harbour Commissioners and renamed *Foyledale* in 1980. She was sold in 1994 to McKenzie Marine UK Ltd, Ullapool, who refurbished her and put her to work around the UK coast as *Ulla Pull*. In 1999 she passed to West African interests as *Luba*.

(Danny Lynch)

This image of the **St. Woolos** provides a good view of her profile and clearly shows her small wheelhouse, short mast and large lifeboat davit partly obscuring her funnel. From the mid-1960s, the British Transport Dock Board's three motor tugs were largely confined to duties within the confines of Newport docks. However, they occasionally ventured out into the Bristol Channel calling at either Cardiff or Barry, and even sailed down to Swansea. This was usually in conjunction with a floating crane or dredger-related movement. It is lunchtime on Tuesday, 4 April 1975, and **St. Woolos** was noted sailing from Cardiff docks, no doubt making her way back to Newport. The **St. Woolos** and her sister **Llanwern** were constructed by P K Harris as twin-screw tugs which made them useful dock tugs as they were quite manoeuvrable. They were for many years, the only tugs in south-east Wales capable of fire-fighting. Like so many tugs from this shipyard, they incorporated a hydroconic design hull, which featured a double-chine and few traditional curved plates. Unfortunately, they were rather unpopular with crews, as they were particularly uncomfortable in heavy seas.

(the late John Wiltshire)

HMS *Wakeful* was a tug with a special role and is seen at Cardiff on 20 September 1979. She was built in 1965 by Cochrane & Sons Ltd, Selby, as *Herakles* for Swedish owner Neptun Bergnings och Dykeri A/B at Stockholm. She was a powerful single-screw tug of 492grt with a bollard pull of 62 tonnes and speed of 14 knots. In 1968 she passed to Göteborgs Bogserings og Bärgnings AB, Göteborg, as *Dan*. She was purchased by the Ministry of Defence (Navy), London in 1974 and in April that year commissioned as HMS *Wakeful* (pennant number A 236). She was assigned to HMS Neptune naval base at Faslane on the Clyde as a submarine escort ship and exercise target. She was also available for use as a fishery protection vessel. HMS *Wakeful* was de-commissioned in October 1987 and sold in May 1988 to Megalahori Hellenic Tugboats, Piraeus, for use as a tug. She was initially registered as *Aegeon Pelagos* which was later amended to *Aegean Pelagos*. She was still at work in 2017.

(the late John Wiltshire)

Cory Towage had established a small tug unit at Plymouth in 1972 when they took over the business of W J Reynolds Ltd. Initially two tugs, *Falgarth* and *Plymgarth* (ex *Thunderer*) were based here along with two launch tugs. These were replaced in 1980 by the 1960-built sister ships *Avongarth* from Avonmouth, and *Plumgarth* from Cardiff. The *Plumgarth* was sold in 1985 and *Avongarth* was increasingly used for coastal towing. She is noted here in the Roath Basin at Cardiff on 15 August 1988 and preparing to tow away the sand dredger *Bowqueen*

to Portugal. In August 1989 it was announced that the Plymouth base would be closed down, and so at 29 years of age, the *Avongarth* was surplus and sold to Holt Associates International (MacGinnity & Wiltshire), Totnes, who renamed her *Tiverton*. This was short-lived as in 1990 she passed to Portuguese owners Bolinhas e Bolinhas as *Galito*. By 2000 and still in Portugal, she was with LUTAMAR of Setubal as *San Vicente*, and working in the Lisbon area. She was broken up in 2006.

(Andrew Wiltshire)

In south-east Wales, West Coast Towing undertook towing work [at] Cardiff, Barry and Newport, but the tugs were normally kept at the latt[er]. As we have seen earlier in the book, from 1994 West Coast gained t[he] contract for ship handling at Port Talbot. The twin-screw *I. B. Smith* w[as] completed at Gorokhovetskiy Shipyard in Russia in early 1992 as *Vik[...]* to a standard Gorokhovets design but was not used as the Soviet Uni[on] had just been dissolved in late 1991. By 1993 she was with Aroco A[...] Stavanger, and was renamed *Vic IV*. She passed to West Coast Towi[ng] (UK) Ltd, Swansea, in 1994 as *I B Smith*, and was one of five simi[lar] tugs purchased that year to replace older tonnage in the West Coast fle[et]. The *I B Smith* was a fire-fighting tug that had been constructed to wo[rk] in ice. She was powered by a pair of 8-cylinder Ruskiy diesels deliveri[ng] 1604bhp which gave her a speed of 11½ knots and a bollard pull [of] 25 tonnes. The *I B Smith* is seen working at Cardiff on 8 June 1994. S[he] was not included in the Wijsmuller takeover in May 2001, and remained w[ith] West Coast Towing until sold to Al Jaber Shipping, Abu Dhabi, in 2005 [as] *Al Jaber VII*.

(Nigel Jone[s])

The British Transport Docks Board was privatised in 1983 and Associated British Ports (ABP) was created. The dredging fleet in South Wales was soon modernised and as part of this process, it was decided to introduce bed-levelling within the dock systems. A suitable tug would be needed to tow the bed-levelling sledge. The *Al Khubar 3* was one of four identical twin-screw tugs completed in Japan during 1976 for International Leasing Co, Sliedrecht, for use in the Persian Gulf. The *Al Khubar 3* was soon sold and sank at Al Jubail, Saudi Arabia, in 1978. She was raised and brought to the Clyde by 1983. Here she was repaired at the old Scott yard at Bowling initially by SB Offshore-Bowling Base Ltd. In 1986 the *Al Khubar 3* was purchased by ABP and arrived at Newport to be modified for her role towing the bed-levelling sledge. She was renamed *Flat Holm* and registered at Cardiff. In this view taken on 14 December 1986 *Flat Holm* is hard at work in the Queen Alexandra Dock at Cardiff. The *Flat Holm* continued in this role, occasionally working away from South Wales at other ABP ports. In 1996 the ABP's dredging operation was renamed UK Dredging and *Flat Holm* became *UKD Flat Holm*. In 1999 she was sold to Coastline Surveys Ltd, Falmouth, and is still at work in 2018 as a survey vessel.

(the late John Wiltshire)

The *Sovereign* is a sistership to *Goliath* seen on page 44 of this book. She was the final tug in a series of four vessels completed in 1956/57 for the Manchester Ship Canal Co from the yard of P K Harris & Sons Ltd, Appledore. She was delivered in February 1957 as *M.S.C. Sovereign* and worked as a ship-handling tug on the canal until laid up by the early 1980s. In 1984 she was sold to Binof Construction, Liverpool, and on to Riverway Developments Ltd as *Sovereign* later the same year. In 1988 she passed to Carmet Tug Co Ltd, Port Penrhyn and Barnton, and this is the period during which we see her off Penarth on 21 April 1991. In 1995 she was sold to Marine Blast Ltd, Belfast, and renamed *MB1* two years later. She moved on to Tyne Towage, Hebburn, in 2001, passing to Svitzer Marine in 2003. Svitzer did not operate the *MB1* which was by now in poor condition. She was resold to Graham Simpson, Newcastle, in 2004 and remained laid up on the Tyne until she was finally broken up in 2006.

(Danny Lynch)

The tidal range in the Cardiff bay area was such that large areas of mud were exposed at low water. This was considered to be a very unattractive feature and so it was decided to develop the waterfront area as a tourist attraction. The solution was a tidal barrage between Cardiff docks and Penarth Marina into which the rivers Taff and Ely would flow. This major civil engineering project was constructed between 1994 and 2001 and was just over 1km in length. It incorporated three locks and a fish pass and quite a few tugs were involved in its construction. One of these was *Zwerver I* which is seen sailing from Cardiff on 8 July 1995. Behind the tug is an early glimpse of barrage construction while in the distance we see the Butetown viaduct crossing the River Taff. The *Zwerver I* is a small twin-screw tug that was constructed in 1994 by Scheepswerf & Reparatiebedrijf Harlingen BV at Harlingen in the Netherlands for Hans van Stee Sleepdienst BV, Harlingen. She had a bollard pull of 13 tonnes and was powered by a pair of 6-cylinder Cummins diesels of 1014bhp. In 2019 she can be found at work in the Caspian Sea sailing as *Caspian Eva* under the Kazakhstan flag for Caspian Services Inc. She has been working on the world's largest lake since 2002, serving the offshore oil and gas industry.

(Nigel Jones)

The **Point James** was a powerful fire-fighting tug built for a specific contract. She was completed in 1972 by Richard Dunston (Hessle) Ltd for service with Smit & Cory International Port Towage Ltd at the Come-By-Chance oil refinery in Newfoundland, Canada. She served here with her sister **Point Gilbert** and two other slightly larger tugs. When the refinery closed, **Point James** and **Point Gilbert** returned to the UK in 1979/80 and took up duties at the newly-opened Royal Portbury Dock near Avonmouth, which required larger and more powerful tugs. The **Point James** boasted a bollard pull of 37 tonnes and was powered by a 12-cylinder English Electric diesel engine of 2640bhp.

This view was taken on 29 August 1993, and **Point James** has come across the Bristol Channel to help out at Cardiff. The following year she was transferred to Belfast and in January 1996 was abandoned and almost lost near Murlough Bay in County Antrim after suffering an engine failure in bad weather. She was recovered and placed back in service at Belfast, eventually passing to Wijsmuller in 2000. In 2002 she was sold to Italian buyer Fenice Services de Transporte Maritimo Lda and renamed **Saint James**. She later passed to Fenwick Maritime SA, Aliaga, Turkey, in 2005 under the Panamanian flag, and was broken up there in 2009.

(Nigel Jones)

The *Zar IV* was an interesting little tug that first appeared in the Cardiff area in 1995. She was quite old but had been rebuilt on a number of occasions. The steam tugs *Zar III* and *Zar IV* were built in Germany in 1913 and 1914 respectively by Schiffswerft und Maschinenfabrik AG, Hamburg for Carl C Zimmermann, Hamburg. They had a gross tonnage of 25, an overall length of 57 feet and were powered by a compound steam engine of 200ihp. The *Zar III* was lost in 1943, while the *Zar IV* continued to work, receiving a 430bhp MWM diesel engine in 1958. She was rebuilt in 1968 by Johann Oelkers of Hamburg and eventually passed to Hans E W Berndt, Hamburg, in 1994. She was immediately resold to a Dutch owner the same year, and came to the UK in 1995 having been purchased by Cardiff Commercial Boat Operators Ltd. In this view *Zar IV* is in Cardiff Bay on 18 February 1995. By 2001 she had moved across to Ireland for service with Bere Island Ferries Ltd of Castletownbere, Bere Island, and was with Shamus Dennehy, Cork in 2003. It is thought she was still going strong in 2011, but has not been heard of since then.

(Nigel Jones)

The first **Bargarth** is featured on page 39 of this book. The second tug to bear this name was an entirely different sort of tug and did not arrive in South Wales until much later in her career. She was originally one of a pair of Voith Schneider tractor tugs ordered by Cory Ship Towage for service at Grangemouth with Forth Tugs Ltd. They were delivered as **Carron** and **Laggan** from the yard of Scott & Sons (Bowling) Ltd on the Clyde. The **Laggan** was the last tug completed by this shipbuilder. She became **Forth** in 1987 after the sale of an older tug released this name. Both tugs were fitted for fire-fighting from new, and had a bollard pull of 24 tonnes. Forth Tugs Ltd was absorbed into Cory Towage Ltd in 2000, which was then taken over by Wijsmuller Marine and subsequently Svitzer Marine Ltd. In 2002 **Forth** was transferred to south-east Wales and was renamed **Bargarth** in 2003. This image of her has been taken from the Cardiff Bay barrage as she sailed from Cardiff on 3 May 2004. She was sold to Tuskar Shipping Gibraltar Ltd in 2009, to be managed by Fastnet Shipping Ltd, Waterford. She was at work with Fastnet in 2019.

(Nigel Jones)

The Avonmouth-based tug *Lowgarth* is heading for the lock in the Queen Alexandra Dock Cardiff on 18 November 1996. She is very smartly turned out in the final version of the Cory Towage livery complete with Cory emblems on her wheelhouse and house flag flying from her mast. The *Lowgarth* was originally based at Cardiff from 1965 until 1979, and then moved across to Avonmouth where she remained until 1997. Being the smallest tug at the port, she was the preferred choice for any towing jobs up the River Severn to Sharpness, which may explain why she lasted as long as she did. She was sold to Willam Faulkner of Northwich in 1997, for recreational use on the River Weaver. Some conversion work was undertaken but she was found to be too big for this role. She then passed to Rigg Shipping, Ipswich, in 2002, and was put back into working condition as a tug. In late 2006 she sailed out to Nigeria as *Charles Plane* under Honduras registry to work for Fendercare Nigeria Ltd. By 2010 she was reported to be with FCN Trident Chambers, Monrovia, and under the Tanzanian flag.

(the late John Wiltshire)

In May 2014 the Royal Navy's Type 45 destroyer HMS **Dragon** made a courtesy visit to Cardiff's Roath Basin and Serco Denholm Marine Services Ltd sent two of their tugs, **SD Independent** and **SD Indulgent**, around from Portsmouth to assist with the docking of the destroyer. Then in the following September the same tugs returned to Cardiff to assist with the docking of Type 45 destroyer HMS **Duncan** in conjunction with the NATO summit being staged in the city. This is **SD Indulgent** on the second occasion. It should be noted that her fendering has been fitted with white covers so as not to mark the warship's hull. In more recent times the superstructure and funnel colours of these two Serco Denholm tugs has been changed to white.

(Marko Waite)

The **SD Independent** and **SD Indulgent** were part of a major tug fleet upgrade within Serco Denholm, and this pair were built to the Damen ASD Tug 2509 standard design. The **SD Indulgent**, the first of the pair, was delivered to her owner in October 2009. Her hull was constructed in Poland by Stocznia Tczew Sp. z o.o. at Tczew, and she was completed by Scheepswerf Damen BV at their Gorinchem yard in the Netherlands. Like her sister tug, the **SD Independent** has a gross tonnage of 186 and is powered by two Caterpillar diesels driving a pair of Aquamaster propulsion units. She is a versatile tug with a useful bollard pull of around 40 tonnes and a fire-fighting capability. This view of the **SD Independent** shows her handling one of the Type 45 destroyers in Roath Basin.

(Paul Andow)

The SMS Towage Ltd tugs are normally based at Newport as this is where the majority of their work is generated. However, they can be seen at Cardiff or even Barry on occasions. A number of the tugs in the SMS fleet came from Hong Kong and were built in Japan in the late 1980s. The *Tradesman* is one such example and she is seen here arriving at Cardiff from Barry on 26 August 2019, after having berthed the tanker *Stolt Shearwater*. She was built in 1987 by Imamura Shipbuilding Co Ltd, Kure, as *Waglan* for Hong Kong Salvage & Towage Co Ltd. She is an ASD tug with a pair of stern-mounted Niigata Z-peller units which give her a bollard pull of 40 tonnes. She is powered by two 6-cylinder Niigata diesels of 2210bhp and she has a gross tonnage of 182. In 2003 the *Waglan* along with her sister *Tai Tam* passed to SMS Towage Ltd, Hessle, and were renamed *Tradesman* and *Trueman* respectively. They were soon put to work on Humberside.

(Bernard McCall)

Our final port is Newport. Newport Screw Towing was founded by Joseph Holman Dunn and had its origins back in 1883 when he acquired his first tug, the *Conqueror* of 1876, which he owned until 1890. He was also a partner in the Prairie Screw Towing Company from 1883 until it ceased to trade in 1896. The Newport Screw Towing title came into being around 1913 when Dunn purchased his second tug, the *Storm Cock* of 1881. The Dun prefix to naming was introduced in 1938. This is the *Dunhawk* of 1943 which Newport Screw Towing acquired in 1960, and is seen off Newport. She was completed on North Humberside by Henry Scarr at Hessle as *Empire Maisie* for the Ministry of War Transport. She was a Birch-class Empire tug having a triple-expansion steam engine with an output of 1000ihp. In 1947 she passed to Clyde Shipping Co Ltd as *Flying Typhoon* and was based on the River Clyde, until her move to Newport. In 1968 *Dunhawk* was replaced by a motor tug and passed to local shipbreaker John Cashmore Ltd.

(Danny Lynch)

Newport Screw Towing operated three Empire-type tugs. The first was *Duneagle* which was a coal-burner and joined the fleet in 1958. She was the first to be sold and went for further service in 1965. The *Dunfalcon* was the last one to enter service doing so in 1961. She was one of the first Empire tugs completed, being an example of the Warrior class. She was built in 1941 on the Clyde as *Empire Pine* by Scott and Sons, Bowling, for the Ministry of War Transport. After the war she remained on the Clyde having passed to Steel & Bennie Ltd in 1946 as *Vanguard*.

Like *Dunhawk*, the *Dunfalcon* had an oil-burning boiler. They operated with a crew of six comprising master, mate, engineer, fireman and two deck boys. In this view *Dunfalcon* is working with the motor tug *Dunsnipe* sailing the cargo ship *Irish Maple* from Newport on a gloomy 2 March 1968. By the late 1960s *Dunfalcon* was the reserve tug and your author saw her working on only two occasions. She was broken up alongside *Dunhawk* on the banks of the River Usk at Newport.

(the late John Wiltshire)

75

John Cashmore Ltd commenced breaking up ships on the banks of the River Usk in 1872, and dealt with well over 1000 vessels of all shapes and sizes until the shipbreaking part of the business ceased in 1976. Quite a few local tugs were dismantled at Cashmore's wharf including the Cardiff tugs *Nethergarth* and *Yewgarth* and Newport tugs *Dunfalcon* and *Dunhawk*. The *Bristolian* was an Avonmouth steam tug that had arrived at the the yard on 1 February 1968. This view of her was taken on 10 March 1968. She was built in 1911 by John Cran & Co, at Leith for the Bristolian Steam Tug Co Ltd (C J King & Sons Ltd) to whom she was delivered in March that year. She had a gross tonnage of 174 and an overall length of 100 feet. Her machinery consisted of a compound steam engine from the shipyard. This had a nominal horsepower of 110, which would have been in the region of 650-700ihp for a steam engine of this period. The *Bristolian* continued her frontline towing duties at Avonmouth until 1964, when she became a reserve tug, having been replaced by the motor tug *Sea Merrimac*. A further new motor tug, *Sea Challenge*, was delivered to C J King & Sons in late 1967, and *Sea Alarm* then became the reserve tug. The *Bristolian* was thus sold for scrap.

(the late Les Ring)

The British Transport Docks Board had three motor tugs at Newport which were used to move ships between the lock and the berth and vice versa. The *Newport* was the oldest of the three and was the first ship-handling motor tug in South Wales. She was a single-screw tug built by W J Yarwood and Sons in 1956 for the British Transport Commission at Newport. The *Newport* was powered by a 5-cylinder British Polar diesel of 700bhp and had a speed of 10 knots. From 1963 the black funnel with a yellow band was replaced with a light blue funnel with a black top. This view of *Newport* was taken in the main lock at Newport in August 1968. She carried the latest funnel colours using a darker blue with the bollard motif, but had yet to receive a beige-coloured hull. During the 1970s *Newport* saw less use and was not included in the Cory takeover of 1977. She was laid up and sold by the BTDB to Egyptian owners in 1978. That was the last we heard of her.

(Danny Lynch)

The Newport Shipbuilding & Engineering Co Ltd was in difficulties by 1970 but did complete an order for two ferries for Caledonian Steam Packet Co. They were to be used on the Kyle of Lochalsh to Kyleakin service and the first to be completed was *Kyleakin* in July 1970. This ferry was then towed to Greenock by the Steel & Bennie motor tug *Campaigner*. Her onward passage to Loch Alsh was carried out by her sister tug *Wrestler*. The *Campaigner* was a fairly large motor tug of 248grt dating from 1957. She was completed by James Lamont & Co Ltd, Port Glasgow, for Steel & Bennie Ltd, Glasgow, and was powered by a 2-stroke Widdop diesel of 1065bhp. Steel and Bennie were taken over by R & J H Rea Ltd in 1970 and the fleet was transferred to Cory Ship Towage (Clyde) Ltd later that year. The *Campaigner* was sold to Frank Pearce (Tugs) Ltd, Poole, in 1977 who changed her name to *Pullwell Victor*. In 1981 she sailed out to Greece and her named changed to *Marambu* for Atrefs Shipping Co, Piraeus. She then passed to Kappa Maritime Co, Piraeus, in 1984 as *Kappa*, and was in existence until 2004 when she was broken up at Aliaga, Turkey.

(Danny Lynch)

After a lengthy voyage from the Gulf of St Lawrence with the bulk carrier **Manitoba** in tow, the ocean-going salvage tug **Britonia** had just arrived at Newport on 19 July 1969. She had handed her tow over to the local tugs for docking. The **Manitoba** was fully laden with iron ore for discharge at Newport, after which she was taken around to Cashmore's yard for breaking up. The **Britonia** was owned and operated by Overseas Towage & Salvage Co Ltd (OTS), London. Her construction had commenced in North Devon at the shipyard of P K Harris & Sons Ltd, and was completed by Appledore Shipbuilders Ltd in July 1963.

The **Britonia** was not a particularly big vessel at 568grt and had an overall length of 157 feet. Her two-stroke British Polar diesel delivered 1270bhp. Her days with OTS and as a tug came to an end in 1971 when she passed to Decca Navigator Co Ltd (Oil Search Marine Management Ltd) for conversion to a research vessel. She was renamed **Decca Surveyor** and in 1980 was sold to Attacus Investments Ltd, London, and renamed **Bon Entente**. By 2000 she was under Ghanaian registry, and believed to be operating off West Africa with Aquatec Diving Services Ltd.

(the late John Wiltshire)

By the mid-1960s the vast majority of larger ships dealt with at Cashmore's scrapyard were former British naval vessels and all arrived under tow in a decommissioned state. In this view on 5 May 1970 the Ministry of Defence (Navy) tug *Reward* has arrived at Newport with the frigate HMS *Troubridge* and is being assisted by the Newport tug *Dunsnipe*. Just visible in the distance through the mist is the outline of Uskmouth power station. HMS *Troubridge* was originally a T-Class destroyer commissioned in 1943 and converted to a Type 15 frigate in 1957. She was finally decommissioned at Chatham in March 1969. The *Dunsnipe* was owned by Newport Screw Towing and was the sister to the *Duncurlew*, both dating from 1962. Later in May 1970 Newport Screw Towing sold out to R & J H Rea Ltd which saw the Newport tugs pass to Cory Ship towage. The *Dunsnipe* was later renamed *Gwentgarth*.

(Danny Lynch)

Your author witnessed **Dunheron** in action on only two occasions at Newport. She always seemed to be kept in nice condition and at some point had the Newport Screw Towing house flag painted on the front of her wheelhouse. She passed into the Cory Ship Towage fleet in 1970, and is seen here at Newport on 25 May 1970, soon after receiving her new owner's funnel markings. She was transferred to Belfast in 1971, as a tug was needed to replace **Craigdarragh** which had been transferred to Londonderry. The **Dunheron** was obviously not what was required at Belfast as she was small and her place at Belfast was filled by **Dunosprey** from Newport. The **Dunheron** passed to A C Cranes Ltd of Dublin in 1972, and was noted by your author at Birkenhead in November that year. In 1978 she eventually ended up with Carmet Tug Co Ltd, Bromborough, who kept her until 1991. By 1996 she was lying in a breaker's yard at Portsmouth, but was rescued for preservation and renamed **Golden Cross** once again. By 2011 she was up for sale, and after breaking from her mooring at Ardentinny, Loch Long, she was deliberately beached. She was eventually broken up at Rosneath in 2014.

(Danny Lynch)

By 1974 shipbreaking at Newport was in decline and a late arrival was submarine HMS *Tabard*. She has arrived behind *Typhoon* which is seen at anchor off Newport on 14 March 1974. HMS *Tabard* (P342) was a T-Class submarine of Group III that was commissioned in June 1946. She was built at Greenock by Scotts and in 1960 went on loan to the Royal Australian Navy. She was refitted at Sydney in 1961/62 and again in 1964/65 which altered her appearance, and returned to the UK in 1968. She then acted as a static training submarine until her sale for scrap in 1974. The *Typhoon* (A95) was a one-off Royal Navy salvage tug with a gross tonnage of 1034 and a length of 200 feet. She had two 12-cylinder Vee Admiralty Standard Range diesels each of 1440bhp. These were built by Vickers at Barrow and geared to a single controllable-pitch propeller. She was built in Leith by Henry Robb Ltd and completed June 1960 for the Admiralty (Royal Fleet Auxiliary), and later transferred to the Royal Maritime Auxiliary Service as seen here. In 1982 she accompanied the Royal Navy Task Force to the Falkland Islands, and was eventually sold in 1989. The *Typhoon* passed to Petros Shipping Co Ltd of Malta and was renamed *P. Typhoon*. In 1992 she was converted to a trawler and renamed *Somalian Glory* and her subsequent career was somewhat troubled as she operated in Somali waters.

(Danny Lynch)

Being of school age, your author would not normally visit Newport docks on a Monday morning in 1972, but 2 April was Easter Monday and a fine day as well. A real turn up for the books was the use of one of the BTDB dock tugs, the *St. Woolos*, to assist with the arrival of the Italian bulk carrier *Polinnia* on the salt water side of the lock. Apparently this was quite an unusual practice at this time. As Cory only kept two tugs at Newport in 1972, it was inevitable that the day would come when there would be no spare tugs available from Cardiff or Avonmouth. The *Gwentgarth* and *St. Woolos* are acting as stern tugs while *Westgarth* was on the bow. Once the lock had been flooded, the BTDB tugs *Newport* and *Llanwern* took over with the berthing.

(the late John Wiltshire)

It is 19 September 1972 and *Llanwern* is seen berthing the laden ore carrier *Pennyworth* with the help of *St. Woolos* at the stern. This is what the British Transport Docks Board tugs would normally be found doing at Newport. Newport docks was still quite busy at this time with regular imports of iron ore to feed the massive British Steel Corporation works at nearby Llanwern. There were also imports of timber as well as exports of motor vehicles and steel products keeping many of the berths in the South Dock busy. Newport had a larger lock than neighbouring Cardiff and Barry and could handle larger vessels, usually bulk carriers. A blow to the port came in 1975 when iron ore imports ceased, and the Llanwern site began receiving its ore by rail from larger ships at Port Talbot tidal harbour. The tug *Llanwern* takes its name from the small village close to the site of the steel works, while *St. Woolos* is named after a parish in the Stow Hill area of Newport famous for its cathedral and hospital.

(Danny Lynch)

The *Cervia* was completed in 1946 as *Empire Raymond* by Alexander Hall of Aberdeen. Later the same year she passed to William Watkins Ltd, London, and was renamed *Cervia*. She continued to work on the River Thames as a ship handling tug until 1972, latterly working for London Tugs Ltd. By 1973 she was back in service commercially and operated by International Towing Ltd (I.T.L.) of Sittingbourne. In July 1975 *Cervia* is seen in North Dock at Newport towing away the former Great Western Railway floating crane *GWR 30*. This was a 50-ton capacity steam-powered crane, and one of a pair completed in 1944. It would appear the *GWR 30* ended its days working in the Orkney Islands and may still be in existence there. The *Cervia* was eventually retired by I.T.L. and passed to the East Kent Maritime Museum at Ramsgate in 1983, where much work has been done to keep her in presentable condition. The *Cervia* still exists at Ramsgate in 2019, but is in need of funds to maintain her.

(Danny Lynch)

The **Cruiser** was completed in 1959 by T Mitchison Ltd of Gateshead as **Clonmel** for John Cooper (Belfast) Ltd. Together with her sister **Cashel** she was stationed at Cobh near Cork for use at the Whitegate oil refinery. This new facility opened in 1959 and was a joint venture between Shell, Texaco, BP and Esso. These tugs featured hydroconic hulls, but were a little unusual in this respect, as they were single-screw vessels. In 1969 John Cooper was taken over by R & J H Rea Ltd, and in 1970 the Rea fleet passed to Cory Ship Towage Ltd. After nearly fourteen years at Cobh, in 1973 **Clonmel** transferred to Cory Ship Towage (Clyde) Ltd, Glasgow, becoming **Cruiser**. She then transferred to the Newport fleet in South Wales where she worked alongside her sister **Portgarth** (formerly **Cashel**). This pleasing image of **Cruiser** was taken in North Dock at Newport on 7 April 1980. After suffering machinery damage, she was sold to Pounds Marine later in 1980, and resold to Falmouth Towage Co Ltd. After repair **Cruiser** was named **St. Gluvias** and put in twenty years' service at the Cornish port. She was sold by Falmouth Towage in 2003 for further service, and in 2019 was reported to be for sale at Hoo Marina in Kent, pending conversion to a houseboat.

(Danny Lynch)

85

Falmouth Towage sent their tug **St. Agnes** from Falmouth to collect the **Cruiser** from Newport. The **St. Agnes** was an interesting tug having been completed in 1935 by Scott & Sons (Bowling) Ltd as the steam tug **Warrior** for Steel & Bennie Ltd, Glasgow. She had an overall length of 114 feet and was powered by a 1000ihp triple expansion steam engine built by Aitchison, Blair, which gave her a speed of 12 knots. She was the first tug on the River Clyde to be fitted with a wireless, and was the vessel on which the Warrior class Empire-type tug was based (see page 75). The **Warrior** was converted to a motor tug in 1958 when her owner had a 7-cylinder Widdop diesel of 930bhp installed. In 1968 she was sold to Falmouth Towage Co Ltd, having been replaced on the Clyde by the new motor tug **Chieftain**. Her new owner renamed her **St. Agnes** in 1969. This view was taken on 7 November 1980 as the pair left Newport for Falmouth. The **St. Agnes** was sold to a shipbreaker at Sittingbourne in 1985.

(Danny Lynch)

In the 1970s Cory sent quite a few tugs to Sharpness for drydocking. From the 1980s onwards Bailey's drydock at Newport picked up a lot of this work, and was quite busy at times. Many of the tugs were local while others like **Seanaid** had come some distance for attention. She was based at Limerick at this time under Irish registry and is seen underway in South Dock on 28 April 1983. The **Seanaid** was one of Rea's three R-class tugs delivered to Milford Haven in 1964/65. She was built by Richards (Shipbuilders) Ltd, Lowestoft, as **Ramsgarth**, and delivered to her owner on 10 September 1964. She passed to Cory Ship Towage in 1970 and was replaced at Milford Haven in 1977 by a new tug. All three R-class were transferred to the Clyde and **Ramsgarth** was renamed **Forager** in 1978 and fitted for fire-fighting. Moving to the west coast of Ireland, she became **Seanaid** in 1981 and in 1986 became part of Cory subsidiary Irish Tugs Ltd. In 1994 she was sold to Intermarine Services SA (Seabulk Shipping SA) as **Pali** under Panamanian registry, and was last heard of in 2007.

(Danny Lynch)

By the early 1970s containerisation was firmly established in the UK shipping industry, and in anticipation of this trade coming to Newport, a large container-handling crane was erected on the north side of the South Dock. However, by 1978 it was quite clear that Newport had missed out as a port, and the crane was disposed of. On 1 April 1978 the **Lady Moira** has been given the task of towing away Lutgens & Reimers' pontoon **P5** complete with the container crane on board. The **Lady Moira** was the first of a pair of powerful tugs completed by Cochrane Shipbuilders Ltd, Selby, for use on the Humber. She had a gross tonnage of 348 and a bollard pull of 40 tonnes. She was delivered to United Towing (Yeoman) Ltd, Hull, and managed by Humber Tugs Ltd. In 1988 her registered owner was Humber Tugs Ltd, Grimsby. Humber Tugs became Howard Smith (Humber) Ltd in 1996, and the following year **Lady Moira** was sold to Multraship BV, Terneuzen, as **Multratug 7**. In 2011 she was chartered to MTS Group Ltd, Falmouth, and renamed **MTS Viscount**. She was back in Newport in August 2018 as **MTS Viscount**.

(the late John Wiltshire) 87

The **5 De Septiembre** was a small tug that was built in the UK and shipped overseas as deck cargo on board the heavy-lift ship **Starman Asia**. It is assumed that the **5 De Septiembre** sailed to Newport from her builder Richard Dunston Ltd in Yorkshire. She was completed in June 1983 at their Thorne shipyard on the Stainforth & Keadby Canal to the order of the Cuban Government. The **5 De Septiembre** is a twin-screw tug of approximately 100 tons gross and with a length of 84 feet. Her main engines consist of a pair of 6-cylinder Mirrlees-Blackstone diesels with a combined output of 824bhp, and driving fixed-pitch propellers. In this view she is now in place on board the **Starman Asia**, and we can clearly see that she has open propellers without Kort nozzles. It is reported that in 1992 she passed to Empresa Constructora de Obras Maritimas del Micons (Ministry of Construction), Havana, as **Astimar X**. More recent photographic evidence would suggest that she is once again sailing as **5 De Septiembre** in Cuban waters as recently as 2017.

(Paul Andow)

The Royal Maritime Auxiliary Service (RMAS) tractor tug **Bustler** (A225) was another visitor to Newport on 3 April 1995 for drydocking. She was the second of the four Adept-class twin-unit Voith Schneider tugs introduced in the years 1980-82 for handling the three Invincible-class aircraft carriers at Portsmouth and Devonport. Her sisters were **Adept**, **Capable** and **Careful** and all were constructed by Richard Dunston (Hessle) Ltd and were capable of fire-fighting. They had a bollard pull of 29.6 tonnes and a speed of 12 knots. These were big harbour tugs with a length of 105 feet, a beam of 31 feet and a gross tonnage of 384. The **Bustler** was delivered in April 1981 and was based at Portsmouth. From 2003 the RMAS tugs were managed by Serco Denholm Marine Services Ltd for the Ministry of Defence and in 2008 **Bustler** passed to SD Marine Services Ltd and was renamed **SD Bustler**. With a new fleet of tugs being introduced from 2007 onwards the **SD Bustler** was laid up and eventually sold. In 2019 she was working in the Gulf of Guinea under the Cameroon flag as **TC Bustler**.

(Danny Lynch)

The **Oliver Felix** was originally an Avonmouth tug, but in subsequent years her history became quite complex and she was sent for breaking on at least three occasions. She was built as **Polgarth** by Charles Hill & Sons Ltd, Bristol, in 1962 and was the first of a pair for R & J H Rea Ltd to be based at Avonmouth to replace steam tugs. In 1970 she passed to Cory Ship Towage Ltd and in 1987 was sent to work at Foynes in Ireland. She returned to Avonmouth and was reported sold to Samuel Evans & Sons, Widnes, in a deal that may have not been completed. She was eventually resold to Divemex Ltd, Newtown, Powys for seabed cable trench ploughing and renamed **Oliver Felix**. Due to a tug shortage at Newport she was chartered to Cory Towage Ltd in 1990/91. Here she is in the South Dock at Newport on 22 January 1990. The **Oliver Felix** was sold by Divemex in 1995 and her subsequent history is chequered. She was detained at Lowestoft by the Maritime & Coastguard Agency in 2000 with numerous defects, but allowed to sail to Southampton for demolition, which did not take place. In 2003 she was again sold for breaking, but then passed to an owner in Plymouth by 2005. By 2007 she was renamed **Luvly Jubly** and **Oliver Felix** again in 2008. She was then finally recycled at Portsmouth in 2011.

(Danny Lynch)

The **Jerome Letzer** is seen here in the early morning sun sailing from Newport with the Ebbw estuary in the background. She had arrived in port on 11 October 1990 with the Belgian jack-up rig **Tijl 1** in tow. She had been on charter from her owner U.R.S. (Unie van Redding en Sleepdienst) to Scheldt Towage Co, Antwerp, since October 1988. The **Jerome Letzer** was completed for U.R.S. in 1974 at Calais by Société Calaisienne with a gross tonnage of 304 and an overall length of 114 feet. She was powered by a 9-cylinder Atlas-MaK diesel of 2600bhp which gave her a bollard pull of 34 tonnes. In 2001 she struck a submerged object while working off Shetland and sustained serious damage to her hull. She was then laid up at Dundee until sold to Med Express Inc (Dick van der Kamp Shipsales BV). She was soon resold to Van Heyghen, Ghent, for breaking up.

(Danny Lynch)

When West Coast Towing Company established its base at Newport they did so with four second-hand tugs that were of East German origin. They were originally placed under the Honduran flag and were named **Aquarius A**, **Pisces L**, **Scorpio N** and **Taurus II**; all were built in the 1970s. Three of them were then given new names in 1994; the **Taurus II** becoming **Hurricane H** and placed in UK registry. She had been completed in the U.S.S.R. in 1977 as **Arni** by Gorokhovetskiy Sudostroitelnyy Zavod and was delivered to VEB Bagger-, Bugsier- und Bergungsreederei, Rostock. A twin-screw tug, she was powered by two Russkiy four-stroke diesels of 1200bhp driving a pair of controllable-pitch propellers, which gave her a speed of 11 knots. The **Hurricane H** is seen off the mouth of the River Usk on a very pleasant 22 July 1995. West Coast obtained some newer tugs of a similar design by 1995 and **Hurricane H** was sold to Peruvian owner Trabajos Maritimos SA (Tramarsa) and was renamed **Tramarsa 3**. She was based at the port of Matarani in Peru and received new 16-cylinder Detroit engines in 1998. She is believed to be still in service.

(Nigel Jones)

The *Gwentgarth* was usually based at Newport with near sister *Emsgarth*, and both tugs regularly worked at Cardiff and Barry when required. This view of her in a lively sea off the Wentlooge levels makes an interesting comparison with the view of her on the front cover in her original Cory livery. Built at Emden in 1972 as **Norderney** for service at this German port, she was a compact and powerful tug with conventional propulsion. Her owner Ems Schlepper AG specified a 22-tonne bollard pull tug with a fixed-pitch propeller enclosed in a Kort nozzle.

She was powered by a 6-cylinder MWM diesel of 1300bhp and had a flying bridge. When she joined the Cory fleet in 1983 she was the second tug to bear the name **Gwentgarth**, the previous example having been sold in 1980. Upon her sale in 1997 she worked in Spain as **Remmar** for eight years before passing to a Russian owner as **Triton**. In 2019 she can be found at work with the Northern Shipping Company in the icy waters around Archangel in northern Russia.

(Danny Lynch)

Shortly after the sale of *Gwentgarth*, the *Holmsider* arrived at Newport from the Tyne fleet. Although much newer than *Gwentgarth*, she was marginally smaller and less powerful with a bollard pull of around 18 tonnes. The *Holmsider*, delivered in June 1984, was the third tug in a series of four conventional single-screw motor tugs built by Richard Dunston at Hessle for service with Lawson-Batey Tugs Ltd. In April 1983 Clyde Shipping Company bought out Lawson-Batey Tugs Ltd, but from 1995 ownership of the Tyne fleet passed to Cory Towage Ltd. The *Holmsider* was soon renamed *Wyegarth* and registered in Newport, as seen here out in the Bristol Channel off St. Brides. Her stay in south-east Wales was to be a brief one, as in June 1998 she was sold to Karapiperis Towage, Salvage and Maritime Co, for further service in Greek waters. After bearing the new name *Karapiperis 15*, she became *Evripos IV* in April 2019.

(Danny Lynch)

The *Vanguard* is seen off Newport with her tow on 16 July 2000. She was another of Rea's R-Class tugs that were delivered new to Milford Haven in 1964/65 (see page 86 lower). The *Vanguard* was launched on 22 October 1964 as ***Rathgarth*** by Richards (Shipbuilders) Ltd, Lowestoft, the last of the trio. She had a gross tonnage of 306 and an impressive length of 127 feet. Her main engine was a 6-cylinder Mirrlees National diesel of 1300bhp which gave her a bollard pull of 22 tonnes and a speed of 11 knots. It should be noted that none of the R-Class was fitted for fire-fighting when built. She passed to Cory Ship Towage Ltd in 1970 and transferred from Milford to the Clyde in 1977 as ***Campaigner***. The rapid decline in shipping on the Clyde saw her move to Irish Tugs Ltd in 1988 as ***Kenry***. She was based at Foynes and replaced *Polgarth*. She was sold to Samuel Evans for scrap in 1991, but resold to Carmet Tug Co Ltd, Barnston, who renamed her ***Vanguard***, and fitted a large towing winch. She became a familiar sight around the UK coast for a number of years until she got into trouble on 7 September 2004. She had to be beached on the island of Rona in the inner Hebrides after she started to sink. A total loss, she was laid up at nearby Kyleakin in 2005, and towed away for recycling in 2010, a sad end to a fine tug.

(Danny Lynch)

The **Kincraig** was built in Japan by Matsuura Tekko Zosen KK, Higashino, in 1997 for service with J P Knight (Caledonian) Ltd and was registered in Inverness. She was delivered to her owner in January 1998. The **Kincraig** is an ASD type tug featuring a pair of Niigata Z-Peller ZP-21propulsion units powered by a pair of Niigata 6L25HX diesels giving her a bollard pull of 50 tonnes. She has a gross tonnage of 290 and is also fitted for fire-fighting. Although normally based at Invergordon on the Cromarty Firth in Scotland, **Kincraig** was also involved with coastal towing and contract work around the UK and northern Europe. She is seen outside the drydock at Newport when she was in port for repairs. In 2009 she was sold to SMS Towage Ltd of Hull and renamed **Welshman**. She continued to work on the Humber until ironically transferred to Newport in 2018. At 3600bhp she is one of the most powerful tugs to have been based in the port.

(Danny Lynch)

The **Kingston** had an eventful career. She was built in 1962 as **Sun XXIV** for service on the Thames with W H J Alexander Ltd and was one of the smaller tugs based at Woolwich for service around the Royal Docks. She was a product of the Faversham shipyard of James Pollock Sons & Co and was powered by a 720bhp 4-stroke Mirrlees diesel engine. In 1969 she passed to London Tugs Ltd which was taken over by Alexandra Towing Co (London) Ltd in 1975. Latterly based at Southampton, she was sold in 1990 to Sub Search Marine Services Ltd, Newhaven, and renamed **Kingston** in 1992. From 1997 she was with a Dutch owner who used her for smuggling drugs. Back on the correct side of the law she had passed to J A Evelegh of Southampton by 2001, who put her back to work towing. She is seen at Newport on 17 February 2002 and is towing away the former Portsmouth to Ryde motor ferry **Southsea** of 1948. The owner was then restyled Griffin Towage & Marine (J A Evelegh). From 2003 **Kingston** was rebuilt and upgraded in 2005 with a Kort nozzle and a bow thruster unit. In January 2019 she was still in service.

(Nigel Jones)

HALLGARTH

The *Hallgarth* and her sister *Holmgarth* were the first new tractor tugs to operate in the Bristol Channel. They were delivered to Cory Ship Towage Ltd in December 1979 and were based at Cardiff. Each tug had twin Voith Schneider propulsion units driven by a pair of 6-cylinder Ruston diesel engines. The *Hallgarth* and *Holmgarth* regularly made appearances at Barry, Newport and occasionally ventured over to Avonmouth and Portbury to help out. In the 1990s, *Hallgarth* also spent short periods away on charter, working at both Devonport and Portsmouth naval dockyards. The *Hallgarth* passed to Wijsmuller Marine Ltd in 2000 which was taken over by Svitzer Marine Ltd in 2001. Resplendent in the colours of her new owner Svitzer, we see her at Newport on 1 September 2002, making a dash for the lock. The *Hallgarth* was sold in 2008, passing to Falmouth Towage Co Ltd, and took up her new role in Cornwall bearing the name *St. Piran*. She is still in service in 2019.

(Nigel Jones)

As Svitzer Marine reduced its presence in south-east Wales, SMS Towage of Hull took full advantage of this situation with support from Associated British Ports which allowed them to set up a base in Newport in 2012. From here they could also provide towage at Cardiff and Barry. The SMS tug *Trueman* is seen working at Newport on 23 August 2018. She is assisting the tug *MTS Viscount* which was towing away the former Severn Sands aggregates dredger *Argabay* that had been renamed *Al Gharb*. The *Trueman* was completed in Japan in 1987 by Imamura Shipbuilding Co Ltd, Kure, for Hong Kong Salvage & Towage Co Ltd as *Tai Tam*. She is an Azimuthing Stern Drive (ASD) tug with a bollard pull of 40 tonnes, and is powered by two 6-cylinder Niigata diesels, driving a pair of Z-peller propulsion units. Her sister ship in Hong Kong was *Waglan* which now features in the SMS Towage fleet as *Tradesman*. The *Trueman* was transferred back to the Humber in 2019.

(Danny Lynch)